CENSUS RECORDS FOR SCOTTISH FAMILIES

AT HOME AND ABROAD

by

Gordon Johnson

Cover design by Sheila Beverley

Matthew James
Fraserburgh
Sunday 20d November
1994

Published by the Aberdeen & North East Scotland Family History Society

Published by
Aberdeen & North East Scotland Family History Society
164 King Street
Aberdeen
AB2 3BD
(Tel. 0224 646323)

Printed by Rainbow Enterprises, Unit 2, Saxbone Development Centre, Dyce, Aberdeen.

£6.-

Acknowledgements

The Aberdeen & North East Scotland Family History Society wishes to thank Mr. Johnson for offering to the Society the revised edition of "Census Records for Scottish Families" for one of its publications.

ILLUSTRATIONS

CONTENTS

DIRECTIONS

Respecting the manner in which Entries should be made in this Book.

The process of entering the Householder's Schedules, in this Book, should be as follows:—

The Enumerator should first insert, in the spaces at the top of the page, the name of the Parish, Quoad Sacra Parish, City or Burgh, Town or Village, to which the contents of that page will apply, drawing his pen through all the headings which are inappropriate.

He should then, in the first column write the No. of the Schedule he is about to copy, and in the second column the name of the Street, Square, &c. where the house is situate, and the No. of the house, if it has a No., or, if the house be situate in the country, any distinctive Name by which it may be known.

He should then copy from the Schedule into the other columns, all the other particulars concerning the members of the family (making use if he please of any of the contractions authorised by his Instructions;) and proceed to deal in the same manner with the next Schedule.

Under the last name in any house he should draw a line across the page as far as the fifth column. Where there is more than one Occupier in the same house, he should draw a similar line under the last name of the family of each Occupier; making the line, however, in this case, commence a little on the left hand side of the third column, as in the example on page vi. By the term "House," must be understood "a distinct building, separated from other buildings by party-walls." Flats, therefore, must not be entered as houses.

Where he has to insert an uninhabited house, or a house building, this may be done, as in the example, by writing in the second column on the line under the last name of the last house

inserted, "One house uninhabited," "Three houses building," as the case may be; drawing a line underneath, as in the example.

At the bottom of each page, on the line for that purpose, he must enter the total number of HOUSES in that page, separating those inhabited from those uninhabited or building. If the statement regarding any inhabited house is continued from one page to another, that house must be reckoned in the total of the page on which the first name is entered. He must also enter on the same line the total number of males and of females included in that page.

When he has completely entered all the Schedules belonging to any one Parish or Quoad Sacra Parish, he should make no more entries on the LEAF on which the last name is written, but should write across the page, "End of the Parish [or Quoad Sacra Parish] of ——;" beginning the entry of the next Schedule on the next subsequent LEAF of his book. The same course must be adopted with respect to any isolated or detached portion of a distant Parish; which portion, for the sake of convenience, may have been included in his District. When he has entered all the Schedules belonging to any Burgh, Village, &c., he should make no more entries on that PAGE, but write underneath the line after the last name, "End of the Burgh, [or Village, &c.] of ——;" making his next entry on the first line of the following PAGE.

In this way he will proceed until all his Householders' Schedules are correctly copied into this Book; and he must then make up the statement of totals, at page ii of this Book, in the Form specified. He must also, on page iii, make up the summaries there mentioned, in the Form according to the instructions there given.

INTRODUCTION TO THE SECOND EDITION

The success of the first edition of this work meant that a new edition was required to update and augment the material.

The first edition included a directory of Scottish census holdings in libraries and archives, although not all libraries and archives replied to my enquiries, and some gave very limited information. Fresh enquiries have been made to rectify these omissions, and update the information, with 1891 returns now available in microfilm.

For a considerable amount of extra material relating to pre-1841 census material and listings, I am indebted to Sir Mervyn Medlycott who has assiduously investigated such holdings throughout the U.K. Some repositories seem not to be fully aware of their own holdings, as our separate enquiries have elicited varying results from the same sources. Perhaps increased interest by historians will improve this situation.

The intention of this work is to provide practical guidance in getting the best out of census and similar records, and on where to find them. They are usually microfilm copies, but material prior to 1841 is still being revealed and made available to family researchers. I would like to thank the many librarians and archivists who dealt with my enquiries so patiently, and expressed willingness to assist further; and particularly those who went out of their way to offer additional possible material for inclusion.

The book is designed to be read through, for better overall understanding of the subject, rather than laid out as a reference work, except for the directory at the end. However, headings have been inserted as a guide to sections which may be of particular interest. References have, for simplicity, been incorporated into the text for this edition.

Foreign census sources have also been expanded where possible, particularly USA and New Zealand, and I am most grateful for the helpfulness of both the National Archives and National Library of New Zealand.

Gordon Johnson

SO - WHAT IS A CENSUS?

The dictionary definition of a census is an enumeration of the inhabitants of a place, from the Latin meaning Register. The census was a regular Roman institution, with the two Censors having the duty of preparing a catalogue of the people and their property, so that each person could be assessed for taxation. The prime function of the modern census is instead to produce a statistical summary which can be used by society to improve the efficiency with which it organises its functions. The statistics allow for prediction of need, can chart population migration, and prepare local government for a surge in numbers or a decrease in school rolls or health service demands.

With modern technology available, the Small Area Statistics of the 1981 U.K. census were made available from 1991 on CD-ROM for computer sorting, tabulation, and mapping. The cost of the CD-ROM disks, at a couple of thousand pounds sterling, means that only large institutions are likely to hold these for the present. However, we may in the future see the possibility of similar transfer of statistical data from Victorian census records as another insight into the social and economic life of our ancestors.

Family historians should look at population statistics, as they can help in understanding the changes through which our ancestors lived. The population figures for a village or district can help us trace the development of a community, and see the pressures put on it by additional population. Furthermore, such statistics can show the population in age groups, telling us how many old people or children there were at any time, the average age of the population, or how many of working age.

Webster's 1755 Scottish census, which can be found in Scottish Population Statistics including Webster's Analysis of Population 1755, ed. by James Gray Kyd; (Scottish Academic Press,1952,repr.1975) for example, told me that Craig parish, by Montrose, had a population of 935 Protestants, no Papists, and the population figure included 187 fighting men (which was defined as aged 18-56). That gives some idea at least of the local population structure, which can be combined with details from the Old Parochial Registers [OPR] and other localised documents to allow historians to describe the development of a community.

Statistics can improve our understanding of other sources of information, and show their limitations. For example, we can look at a Bill of Mortality drawn up in Glasgow in 1831: Enumeration of the inhabitants of the City of Glasgow and County of Lanark, 1831.

1

(Glasgow,1832). The compiler wanted the statistics of births to be accurate, so instead of using the baptismal registers, where it then cost a shilling to have a baptism registered, he asked the clergymen to keep a simple register for one year of the number and sex of children actually baptised. That year in Glasgow, he found that 2,370 more children were baptised than were recorded in the church OPRs - nearly half of all the births!

This illustrates a national problem of missing baptisms in the Old Parish Registers. It also reinforces the point that statistics are worth looking at, to put family information into context.

Statistical detail is also available from the census of Religious worship, and of Education, that was taken as part of the 1851 national census in Scotland. It is full of data on the number of churches of each denomination in each county, number of sittings, attendances, and the periods when the churches were built. The education census provides a good insight into the wide range of educational establishments in use in 1851, including Sunday Schools. For literary and scientific institutions, which include societies, there is a list of such bodies by name in each county, with details sufficient to assess the local value of such a body. The Straiton village library in Ayrshire, for example, had 33 members, only one of them female, and there were 580 volumes in the library; in Stirlingshire the Denny & Dunipace Athenaeum provided a course of ten scientific lectures for the sum of 5 shillings. All good background detail for the family historian.

The purpose of a census is to provide statistics, nothing else. So how come we have something we can use for our purposes? The answer is sheer luck, that someone decided that the originals, the source material, might be worth preserving for the future. However, today's archivists and librarians take the positive attitude that historical documents should be preserved for future historians, and fortunately government has managed to agree to the preservation of most documents of this nature, although, in other areas, government officials have done major thinning out to cut down the bulk.

BEGINNINGS

The idea of a national census in the U.K. came early. A religious census was taken by the Church of England in 1676, providing a fair head count of most of the population of England and Wales, with the occasional return giving names. The best available source is The Compton Census of 1676: a critical edition, ed. by Anne Whiteman (London, for the British Academy, O.U.P.,1986).

A full national census gradually became considered and in 1753 a Bill was proposed in Parliament for this purpose. Although it was passed by a large majority in the House of Commons it was rejected by the House of Lords because a census was felt by them to be an infringement of liberty. It was 1801 before the first national British census was taken, and then the intention was "to take an account of the total number of persons within the kingdom of Great Britain." Note that numbers are the object of the exercise.

If you would like to read a bit more about the early censuses, the best work is: Guide to Census Reports, Great Britain 1801-1966 (London, H.M.S.O., 1977).

As far as genealogically useful census documents are concerned, our luck was a bit late in arriving, for, although a census was taken every ten years nationally from 1801, the source material from 1801,1811,1821 and 1831 has not survived, except in a few local cases.

Since 1841, a full national census has been taken, and the detailed information on individuals kept, except for 1941, when the war prevented a census being taken. There was, however, a National Registration of the entire population in 1939, to identify everyone and issue them with identity cards. The way this was done was very similar to a census, and the enumeration books used should be helpful when released, presumably in 2039!

The censuses of 1801 to 1831 were really only intended as statistical exercises, and do not list actual names, but, people being people, some of the enumerators wrote down names so that they knew what they had covered, or for their own interest. When the data was transferred into the official returns book, normally the source material was destroyed. In some cases, through the personal interest of the enumerator, original material was kept and put in a relatively safe place - usually church records.

An example is a notebook by the Minister of Peterhead, George Moir, dated July 1801, listing all the details for answering the census questions. Not only did he carefully tabulate all the necessary answers, he also gives the name of the principal tenant of each property, and at the end gives quite a detailed decription of the parish population size over the years, and notes the failure to register baptisms and marriages in particular periods. The original is now in the safekeeping of North East Scotland Library Service, and a transcript with an added index is now being published by Aberdeen & N.E.Scotland F.H.S.

Other instances have survived where an enumerator did his census in extra depth, listing all the names, etc. The work was then turned into the official format and sent in, with the original, more detailed, version being retained. One example was the 1811 and 1821 census returns for Dunnottar parish, Stonehaven . These were in the Church of Scotland records later deposited in the Scottish Records Office in Edinburgh [Ref.CH2/110/12],in accord with a decision of the General Assembly. Both returns are now available locally on microfilm.

Orkney Archives have a List of Inhabitants for the parish of Orphir, dated 1821, which was among the church records of St. Magnus Cathedral. The list is effectively a census return, giving names, occupations, ages in ten year brackets (5 year for children), relationships, and as a bonus the number of black cattle, sheep, geese, etc., and holdings in boats and farm equipment.

Transcripts of the 1821 returns for the Orkney parishes of St. Andrews, Deerness, Sandwick, and Stromness are held by the Orkney Library Archivist. Those for St. Andrews and Deerness are transcriptions done about 1900 by a William Spence. The originals are believed to be in private hands.

Another transcript with the archivist is the 1821 census of South Ronaldsay, Burray, Swona and Pentland Skerries, done by the S.Ronaldsay parochial schoolmaster, Peter Nicholson McLaren. It gives names and ages at each place, but includes later notes on some individuals. Another typescript copy is held at the Family History Shop in Aberdeen.

1821 and 1831 returns for the Shetland parish of the island of Fetlar are to be found in the Shetland Archives. They give numbers only, but in more detail than appears in the published reports.

Strathclyde Regional Archives have 1821 draft census schedules of Lesmahagow parish, Lanarkshire, naming heads of families and their spouses, with numbers of children and other statistics of the families.

Moray District Libraries have photocopies of mss. censuses (all named) of Mortlach parish (1805 & 1821), Dufftown (1820 & 1826), and Glenrinnes (1801, householders only).

Schoolmaster Peter Forbes' census enumerator's scroll returns for Longforgan, Perthshire, for the years 1811,1821,1831 and 1841 are to be found in the Archive &

Record Centre at Dundee, with the bonus of the 1811 return being indexed. The centre also holds a one volume Population of the Town, 1801, which gives only details of name and district, but is indexed.

Lochwinnoch, Renfrew, 1821, a list of householders, is to be found in a series of bound manuscript volumes called the "Cairn of Lochwinyoch",(Vol.XVIII,p.402) compiled by a housebound doctor of the period. He passed his time noting down facts, relevant and irrelevant, about life in the village. The volumes are held by Paisley Public Library's local history department.

Other survivals whose existence and location have been established include those for Gordon parish, Berwick, 1801,1811,1821,[SRO-CH2/457/2]; Ladykirk and other Berwick parishes for 1811 and 1831,[SRO-CH2/660/4,5]; Jedburgh,[SRO-CH2/552/44] and Melrose, Roxburgh, for 1831,[SRO-CH2/386/19].

St. Quivox, Ayrshire parish population report 1821 [CH2/319/22] and Kirkoswald, Ayrshire, 1831 list of parishioners [CH2/562/27], List of heads of households for Kirkoswald parish, circa 1690 [ATD42/7/6] are among items held by the Ayr sub-office of Strathclyde Regional Archives.

The National Register of Archives (Scotland) surveys archives in private and corporate hands, and among Grant of Rothiemurchus papers recently surveyed [Survey no.102] were a census of Rothiemurchus, circa 1830/40, with considerable detail, and a List of the population in the parish of Rothiemurchus, 1837, based on heads of families. Enquiries about access to these items must be through the N.R.A.(Scotland).

Lists for Lochrutton, Kirkcudbright, 1766, 1821, & 1831, formerly held in the parish, have now been deposited at the SRO [CH2/1344/16, 19 & 20]. Other lists for Moulin, Perth, 1821,[SRO-CH2/488/20]; Ormiston, East Lothian, 1811, 1821, 1831,[SRO-CH2/292/24]; and Stow, Midlothian, 1801, [SRO-GD113/465-7] are all held by the Scottish Record Office.

A similar situation exists for England & Wales. One survival was at Hendon, Middlesex, where enumerators books are now held by the Library Services Archives of the London Borough of Barnet, The Burroughs, Hendon, London NW4 4BG, for the 1801, 1811, and 1821 censuses. They had been stored in a large cupboard with many other documents belonging to the parish.

Then in Berkshire Record Office there is a very detailed set of lists of families prepared for the 1801 census in Binfield. They also have draft returns for Earley for 1821.

Other examples can probably be found in various parts of the U.K., so it is worth making enquiries in local

authority archives (and in England the County Record
Offices). The majority of survivals are to be found in
the Scottish Record Office in Edinburgh, and the Public
Record Office in London. A good descriptive review of
pre-1841 census lists in Britain, although almost all
English examples, is Colin Chapman's: Pre-1841 Censuses
and Population Listings" (2nd edn., FFHS, 1991). A new
publication giving the most comprehensive listing of
locally-produced census records, with Scotland well
covered, is: Local Census Listings, 1522-1930: holdings
in the British Isles, by J.Gibson & M.Medlycott
(FFHS,1992). In the course of research for the present
book, additional censuses have been located, and noted
in the directory section.

LOCAL CENSUSES

Most of the vanished early census returns were so
lacking in detail that they are not really much of a
loss. A very different case is that of Glasgow, where
the man entrusted with running the census in the city
reckoned he knew better what information was needed for
the city's use, and, although he did the official
census, he ran his own, more detailed, local census in
1819.

James Cleland, who had been particularly interested in
death statistics, known as Bills of Mortality, persuaded
the City Council that a Glasgow-wide census would be
invaluable to the city, and provide more detailed
information than was to be provided by the national
census of 1821. The City Council, Police Commissioners,
and Hospital Governors agreed to support his plans.

The enumeration books that were used were to include
"...householders names, their profession, the number and
description of their families, their servants, the names
and profession of their lodgers, the religion they
professed, the country to which they belonged, the
street or land in which they resided, the number of the
house, the length of residence, and all other
circumstances that appeared to deserve notice."

The proposal was well publicised in the local
newspapers, and bill posters, asking for the public's
cooperation by explaining what it was about. The actual
survey was taken between 14 October 1819 and 26 February
1820. When the survey books were returned, everyone was
requested to call at the Superintendent's office and
examine the lists, to remove any doubt about the list-
takers' accuracy in recording the details. The
statistical results were then published as: Statistical
Tables relative to the City of Glasgow, with other
matters therewith connected, compiled by James Cleland
(Glasgow, James Lumsden & Son, 1823)

Unfortunately for us, the enumeration books do not seem
to have survived the passage of time. Neither the
Regional Archives nor the Scottish Record Office have
them, and it can only be assumed that this invaluable
set of returns was destroyed afterwards.

I understand that there was a religious census of
Glasgow done by a man by the name of MacLennan, but here
again only statistics were kept. More useful is the
Cholera Rental Book for 1832 in Glasgow. This volume
contains a list of all heads of families, with their
occupation, by address, who were assessed for a special
rate to pay the costs of a cholera outbreak. This
amounts virtually to a census of households for Glasgow

in 1832-1833. I believe the Glasgow & West of Scotland
F.H.S. are indexing this.

Another local census taken in 1819 was the Burgh Census
of Kirkcudbright. The reason for it is uncertain, but it
lists all adults by name (except wives) with their
occupation, children by name, and whether each
individual is over or under the age of 12, with totals.
The occupation column includes some unhelpful terms,
such as Lodger and Apprentice, but otherwise is clear.
The document is held by the E.A.Hornel Art Gallery &
Library in Kirkcudbright, who hold another item of even
greater interest - a list of the population of the
parish of Balmaclellan in 1792, compiled by the Rev.
James Thomson for use in making his return to Sir John
Sinclair for the First Statistical Account of Scotland.
The list, under farm or estate names, gives the name of
each person in the household, adult or child, with their
exact age, but not occupation. Details of other useful
holdings in the Hornel library are in the directory
section under Kirkcudbright.

A number of other local censuses have managed to
survive, some of which have been published.

The Annan Parish Censuses 1801-1821, ed. by George
Gilchrist (Edinburgh, Scottish Record Society,
1975) publish the records kept by the local schoolmaster
after the statistical information had been provided for
the census officials. For the most part, they provide a
full list of names of persons in each household, but at
a later stage in the 1811 and 1821 census he seems to
have been rushed and ended up abbreviating his returns
to the head of the house, and not naming the other
people there. If you have any relatives from that
vicinity, it is worth perusing this volume. As a bonus
it includes a short list of people for tax assessment in
1798.

Another book of value is The Urquhart Censuses of
Portpatrick, 1832-1853, ed. by N.L.Tranter (Edinburgh,
Scottish Record Society, 1980). These were taken by a
local minister, the Rev. Andrew Urquhart, and are quite
detailed, giving not only names but ages and
occupations, and whether local born - and if not, how
long resident and a few other details. The most detail
comes in his first census, taken over 1832-34, and less
information in the later ones, taken sporadically in
1844, 1846, and 1852.

This and the Annan volume are indexed, making them very
useful for our purposes. However, as this was one man
compiling his census over considerable periods of time,
they should not be considered to be entirely
comprehensive, due to possible "flitting" during the
period.

The difficulties which arise from taking a census over a
period of time, when people may move from place to place

while the census is being taken, existed right up to and including the 1831 census. The 1841 census was the first to be taken on a single day, and so starts to have some degree of accuracy. However, accuracy is relative, and the census takers gradually refined their techniques over the decades, learning from past mistakes.

One problem which eventually showed up was that while in Scotland it was the schoolmaster who was given the job of enumerator in the early censuses, in England it was done by parochial officers and clergymen. The schoolmasters proved much more efficient at the job, and provided more complete and accurate information. The result was that a clear need was established for accurate conduct of the census, so that from 1841 the job was handed over to the Registrar General in England.

The schoolmasters in Scotland continued to take the census in 1841 and 1851, on commission from London, through the agency of the Sheriffs in Counties, and of the Chief Magistrates in Royal and Parliamentary Burghs.

After the 1855 establishment of the civil registration system in Scotland, the Registrar General's department in Scotland took over the census enumeration through the local registrars, and the 1861 census of Scotland was done by 1001 registrars and 8075 enumerators. Although at times there have been minor differences between Scotland and England in the actual schedules, the differences did not at any time prevent tables being compiled on a Great Britain basis.

THE CENSUS OF 1841, AND OTHER DATES TO NOTE

The first generally useful material from the official censuses is that dated 1841, because of its naming of individuals. But even then its usefulness is limited. The 1851 census is the first of the really good ones from our point of view.

You should be aware of the exact census dates, because the date on which the enumeration was taken varied slightly each time. For 1841, it was 7th June; in 1851, it was 31st March; in 1861, it was 8th April; in 1871, 3rd April, in 1881 it was 4th April, and 5th April in 1891.

The 1891 census has now been released on microfilm, and many libraries now hold copies or are in the process of purchasing them as funds permit. The 1901 census returns will not be available for public scrutiny at all until the year 2001. Fortunately, most of us are more interested in the earlier years.

You can write to the Office of Population Censuses and Surveys, St. Catherine's House, 10 Kingsway, London WC2B 6JP, for details of a named individual in the three oldest of the closed registers, provided you can supply that individual's written consent, or prove you are a descendant of the person, and you have to provide the address for the person. A fee is payable for such a service.

FINDING THE CENSUS RETURNS

Where can you see census material, and can you get someone else to check the census for you, for distant places?

To see, in one place, microfilm of returns covering the whole of Scotland, you have to go the Registrar General at New Register House in Edinburgh, where you can consult the microfilm for any place in the country. For England and Wales, the Channel Islands, and the Isle of Man, the place you need is the Public Record Office, which is now located at Chancery Lane, London WC2A 1LR. Mormon Family History Centres can also obtain census microfilm for anywhere in the UK, though this takes time.

One point to note is that the government charges considerable daily fees at both London and Edinburgh for access to these records, whereas libraries and archives holding local microfilm copies generally make no access charge. You should ask about the current fees in force before you go to the PRO or New Register House.

In both Edinburgh and London, printed indexes are readily to hand for all major cities, and some large towns, allowing a quicker guide to the correct film provided you know the street name.

No-one gets to see the original census returns these days. Only microfilm may be consulted in both places. It is also best to arrive early and book your seat, to guarantee your access to a microfilm reader. It is advisable to leave your coat on the seat when you have to leave it, to indicate that it is already in use. Do not leave anything valuable! You can purchase a photocopy of the census page, and this can be valuable and time-saving.

I should explain a little about the Mormon Family History Centres. The Church of Jesus Christ of Latter-Day Saints, better known as the Mormons, provides a worldwide network of church Family History Centres (70 in the UK) primarily for church members, but also generously allowing non-members access. Each Centre holds census microfilm purchased from their national service centre.

Coverage is mainly for its own area, but also for other areas reflecting users' interests, as film obtained may be retained at the centre. Each centre is able to obtain at reasonable cost census microfilm for anywhere that the church has microfilmed, which includes the whole of the UK. There is no central record of holdings, but, from my own experience as a user, local centres can have surprisingly widespread coverage outside their own localities.

Enquiries can be made by telephone to the LDS church in the nearest large population centre, and they will tell you which is the nearest centre to you. As space and opening times are limited, advance booking is essential. Please remember when visiting that the centres are primarily for church members and you are a guest.

THE CENSUS IN SCOTTISH FAMILY HISTORY SOCIETIES
Entries updated:(month/year)

Aberdeen: The Family History Shop, 164 King Street, Aberdeen (from July 1993), Tel.0224-646323, belongs to Aberdeen & North East Scotland Family History Society, and holds 1841-1891 census microfilm for all parishes of Aberdeenshire, Banffshire, and Kincardineshire, plus 1841-1881 for Moray & Nairn; Also 1841 for Inverness, Shetland, Orkney, Caithness, Sutherland, Ross & Cromarty, plus a dozen or so Angus parishes for 1841 and 1851, 3 Inverness parishes in 1861, 6 Wigtownshire parishes, 1851, and Old Monkland, Lanarkshire, 1851. One or two English census microfilms are also held. If a member provides addresses, up to 6 entries can be extracted free of charge from census returns, but searching for a person costs £1 per parish (Aberdeen excluded). The society has on microfiche a name index for the City of London 1851 census; and a number of 1851 indexes for parishes in Aberdeenshire and Banffshire. The society's extensive library holds a fair number of census-related items, including the 1828 census of New South Wales; and 1851 census indexes for many places in England, produced by various family history societies. Quarterly journal, large and expanding range of publications. Holds the latest (1992) IGI for UK & many other countries. This Society has the largest membership in Scotland, and operates a postal bookselling service offering books from many publishers (free list). Membership subs.: Ordinary(U.K.) & Institutional - £10, Overseas, U.K.Student/pensioner - £8, Family - £14. There is also a joining fee of £2.(7/93)

Anglo-Scottish Family History Society (linked to the Manchester & Lancashire FHS.) Secy.: Mrs M.C. Rhodes, Clayton House, 59 Piccadilly, Manchester M1 2AQ. Society library has census microfilm for some Stirlingshire parishes, 1841-1881, and one reel for part of Perthshire, 1851. Also holds extensive range of 1851 census indexes covering large areas of England, especially S-E Lancashire. Publications: Five dictionaries of emigrant Scots, many taken from census returns; Scottish Genealogy: a digest of 295 publications held by Manchester Central Library; Parish and Non-Conformist Registers in Manchester Central Library. Membership subs.: UK - £10; Family - £12.50; European - £12.50; Other overseas - £15. (2/93)

Borders Family History Society. Secy.: Mrs. Carol Trotter, 15 Edinburgh Rd., Greenlaw, Berwickshire TD10 6XF. Newsletter with queries section. 1990 booklet on members' interests. Small library held by Archivist at Borders Regional Library headquarters, St. Mary's Mill,

Selkirk. Roxburghshire monumental inscriptions books published by society: Hownam & Linton, Morebattle, Yetholm, Sprouston & Lempitlaw, Eckford, and Ednam, each £3.50 (members) or £4.50 (non-members) plus postage: UK 50p, overseas airmail £1.50. Membership subs.: Ordinary - £7, O.A.P. - £5. Membership secretary: Mrs. Fay Mackay, Caddonmill, Clovenfords, Galashiels, Selkirkshire.(1/93)

Central Scotland Family History Society, c/o Mrs. E. Lindsay, 28 Craiginnan Gardens, Dollar, Clackmannanshire FK14 7JA, was formed in 1990, and has a steadily growing membership. Membership subs.: Ordinary, Institution, Society or Company - £7.50; Overseas - £10; Retired, student or unwaged - £5. Publications: Bi-annual newsletter with queries section; Stirling Burgess Lists, 1600-1699; 1700-1799; 1800-1902. No census holdings, but 1851 Stirlingshire & Clackmannanshire census is gradually being indexed by members. (2/93)

Dumfries & Galloway Family History Society, c/o Miss Betty Watson, Kylelea, Corsock, Castle Douglas, Kirkcudbrightshire DG7 3DN. c.750 members. No census holdings. Has published 1851 census records by surname, for parishes of Johnstone, Applegarth, Canonbie, Cummertrees, Durisdeer and Balmaclellan.(Applegarth-£1, others £2, plus 40p.p&p UK, 60p surface mail elsewhere, set of 6 £7.50 plus £1.10/£1.70; publishes a newsletter 3 times/year; members interests booklet; sources booklet. Membership subs.: Ordinary -£6, Family -£7.50, Student/pensioner -£5, Overseas -£8. (2/93)

Fife Family History Society, c/o Mrs. Ward, 3 Lochiel Place, Methil, Fife KY8 3JJ, is a recently-formed society.

Glasgow & West of Scotland Family History Society, c/o Mr. Frank Inglis, 3 Fleming Rd., Bishopton, Renfrewshire PA7 5HW. The Society's library is housed within the Mitchell Library, Glasgow, and may be consulted by members by prior arrangement. See the Society's Newsletters for library catalogue. They do not hold their own census microfilm. Society members are currently indexing the 1851 Glasgow census,only partly completed.
Membership subs.: Ordinary - £6, OAP - £3; £3 per extra family member. Institutions - £8.(2/93)

Hamilton District Family History Society, c/o James Wallace, 24 Anderson St., Burnbank, Hamilton ML3 0QJ is a recently-formed society (1991) catering for interests in north and central Lanarkshire. Membership subs.: Individual - £6; Retired, student or unwaged - £3; Overseas - £8. Bi-annual newsletter with members interests, etc.(1/93)

Highland Family History Society, c/o Reference Section, Main Library, Farraline Park, Inverness IVl lNH, has bought microfilm of the 1841-1891 census returns for the counties of Caithness, Ross & Cromarty, Inverness, Nairn, Argyll, Shetland Islands and Orkney Islands. The material is all held at this library, available both to members of the S ociety and the general public. The microfilm readers belong to the library, not the Society. Publications include 1851 census indexes for certain parishes in Ross & Cromarty - Killearnan, Kiltearn, Kincardine (with Croick), Knockbain, and Tain, and in Caithness - Wick (landward). Membership subs.: Ordinary-£6, Family-£8, pensioner-£4, Institutional-£10 (overseas members, add £2 for airmail postage of journals). (2/93)

Scottish Genealogy Society. Library & Family History Centre at 15 Victoria Terrace, Edinburgh EHl 2JL (tel.031-20-3677). Holdings include census microfilm 1851 and 1861 for Edinburgh; Scot, Wm. - parish lists of Wigtonshire and Minnigaff; Davidson, F. - Examination Roll of Arbroath, 1752, and Town's Duty Roll, 1753. Quarterly journal "Scottish Genealogist". Descriptive leaflet on Society. Library may be consulted free by members of affiliated societies, others are charged £1 per visit to use facilities. Large holdings of monumental inscriptions, printed and manuscript, some published by the Society. Holds IGI, and fiche indexes to OPRs. Queries to Hon. Librarian, Robert M. Strathdee, 89 Craigleith Road, Edinburgh EH4 2EH.
Membership Secretary, 45 Dick Place, Edinburgh EH9 2JA (UK residents), 15 Victoria Terrace, Edinburgh EHl 2JL (Overseas residents). Membership subs.: £12 (US $24) per annum, Family Membership £15, for 2 named members of a family. (6/93)

Shetland Family History Society, Secretary: Mrs. E.M.Angus, "Seafar", 12a Lovers Loan, Lerwick, Shetland ZEl OBA, was formed in 1991. Holds no census material yet. Publications: Journal - "Coontin' Kin"; Booklet "Tracing in Shetland" due shortly. Membership subs.: Ordinary - £10; Family - £15; O.A.P - £7; Overseas - £15.(2/93)

Tay Valley Family History Society now have their own premises, The Family History Research Centre, 179 Princes St., Dundee DD4 6DQ, Tel.0382-461845. 1841-1891 census microfilm held is mainly Dundee and environs, with more being added. Has an alphabetical index of names for 1841 census of Dundee and some areas around. Has IGI for whole of Scotland, adding rest of UK shortly. Expanding library includes family trees, cemetery lair indexes, M.I.s, pedigree charts. Publishes

regular journal, a local source book, and series of booklets, e.g."Tay Valley People".
Membership subs.: £5 per annum (ordinary), £3 (student/OAP), £6 (family), £7(institution). (3/93)

Troon & District Family History Society, c/o M.E.R.C., Troon Library, South Beach, Troon, Ayrshire KA10 6EF. No census material held. Membership subs.(Aug.-June): £7.50 for UK and £9.50 for overseas members; £9.00 for family membership. Meetings are held on the third Tuesday of each month. Publications include: Members Interests Directory (1992) and Dundonald Mortality Register, and a journal published three or four times per year. Some M.I. publications are in preparation. (1/93)

CENSUS RECORDS IN SCOTTISH LIBRARIES

The directory at the end of this book is based on replies from Scottish public libraries and archives, and here I wish to discuss only certain aspects of coverage, giving a few examples to indicate what you might expect.

For Aberdeenshire, Kincardineshire, Banffshire, and Moray, the local public library services - Moray District Libraries, Aberdeen City Libraries, North East Scotland Library Service - provide almost complete coverage in census microfilm and are improving local access to such material every year. Angus is now well covered and in Dundee the city library has a reasonable collection.

Glasgow concentrates its resources in the Mitchell Library, North St., Glasgow, G3 7DN, and only concerns itself with the city, for which it has complete coverage. Their census microfilm has been placed on open access, along with the street indexes to the films. You can look up the street to identify which film you need, then pick the film from the shelf and take it over to the microfilm reader. Glasgow is fortunate in having a street index for each census year 1841-91, with the street and house numbers related to enumeration district and book no.

Many public libraries throughout Scotland hold microfilm of census records, old parochial registers and newspapers. Kirkcaldy District Libraries published in 1992 their "Genealogical Microform Holdings in Scottish Libraries", covering census and OPR holdings. Any edition is out of date immediately it is published, and the availability of the 1891 census on microfilm from the start of 1992 means that this item may not have been held at the time. The directory at the back of this book brings that further up to date, and includes material not on microfilm.

In the North, The Highland Family History Society owns returns which are housed in the Inverness public library. Orkney has all returns for its area, as well as some censuses for 1821, and the Clan Donald Centre in Skye has 1841-91 census records not only for Skye but also other Clan Donald areas.

Southern Scotland is very variable in coverage, with Borders Region well served and up to date. Dumfries & Galloway Regional Library Service has restricted itself to offering the 1851 census on microfiche at a number of libraries, but 1841-1891 census microfilm for Dumfriesshire, Kirkcudbrightshire and Wigtownshire can be found in the Dumfries Archives Centre.

Some of our university libraries hold census microfilm, but the newer ones have little or nothing in this field. Archives, rather than libraries, normally hold original manuscript material, although some libraries also employ archivists. Most archive material goes to the Regional Council Archivist as a repository of all council documents in the area, and this can sometimes include census documentation. Central Region Archives are good in this respect, holding both census microfilm and earlier census-type documents, while Grampian Region Archives have none of either.

Use the directory at the back of this book as your general guide to what is available for your locality. Please note that libraries and archives can often hold material relating to adjacent geographical areas. If you want to explore for furher material, try asking all the local groups such as local history societies, museums, antiquarian societies. I have not had the time to investigate all these for this book, only a few which came to my notice. Older societies may have back runs of their journals which can include name lists from private sources which no-one else has found: if you discover something worthwhile, please let me know for inclusion in a future edition.

CENSUS HOLDINGS IN SOUTHERN BRITAIN

A useful general work is J.S.W. Gibson's "Census Returns 1841-1881 on microfilm: a directory of local holdings in Great Britain; Channel Islands; Isle of Man", now in its 5th edition, 1990, published by the Federation of Family History Societies, and much improved in its Scottish coverage.

Another helpful FFHS publication is "The Censuses 1841-1881 - their use and interpretation, by Eve McLaughlin" The 1988 edition now includes Scotland. It gives good general advice. Most recently, "An Introduction to The Census Returns of England and Wales", by Sue Lumas [FFHS, 1992] gives good guidance to using the returns from 1841 held by the P.R.O. in London.

The Public Record Office also produces a 4-page leaflet on the Censuses of Population 1801-1881, available free of charge, which, while referring to the population of the United Kingdom at the beginning, fails to make clear that the leaflet is not talking about Scotland's returns. Eventually, a small mention is made of "surviving returns for Scotland are held at...".
Should you have need to go to London to research, the Search Rooms for censuses of England and Wales are now located at the Public Record Office, Chancery Lane, London WC2A 1LR (Tel.081-876-3444)

The Essex Society for Family History have also published a little booklet "The census and how to use it", by John M. Boreham,3rd imp. 1987, which is quite helpful in the details of using English census material.

HELP FROM THE LIBRARIES?

What kind of service you get from a public library in searching census records depends on the library policy. This can be influenced by the amount of demand they have. Some libraries have found that catering wholeheartedly to genealogical enquiries results in anything up to three-quarters of all their queries being of this kind.

The general pattern is that the more you ask, the less enthusiastic the library will be. Library staff try to be helpful, particularly to overseas or other distant enquirers, but a five-page letter with detailed lists of puzzles to be solved is not the best way to seek help. Try instead a short note asking for the solution to a single point, or perhaps two. It will likely be answered quickly, and may save you asking some of the other questions if the answers are useful.

Some libraries now limit the amount of time devoted to each query, and go no further; others simply refuse to do "research", saying that it is up to the person to come in, or send someone to do the work. Most, however, strike a balance and will ask locally-based folk to come in, while distant enquirers will be catered for more fully by post, provided they are willing to accept a sometimes considerable delay.

The dearest charges that have come to notice are those of Highland Regional Archive, whose rates for detailed research by their genealogist in residence start at £11.50 for the first hour, although a brief introduction to sources and guidance is free.

Stirling Central Library gives the first half hour of staff time free, than charges £10 per hour for staff reseach in unindexed material or extensive use of other materials. Costs are agreed in advance, based on an initial assessment of likely level of research needed.

North East Scotland Library Service levies a charge of £8.00 per hour for genealogical research done by library staff (beyond an initial half hour which will remain free of charge and which covers most enquiries). Research done in person is free, and appointments to view microfilm and microfiche can readily be made. Provision of microfilm and microfiche readers in local libraries is being extended, and these can mostly be used without appointment. Lists are available showing what census records are available at each local library.

Perth & Kinross District makes a research charge of £10.00 per hour for enquiries originating outside the local authority's area, and people from outwith the District are charged £1.00 per hour for the use of m/f readers.

Dumbarton District Libraries have maintained their charges at £5 per hour for research if local studies staff have to use unindexed material.

North East Fife Libraries now make a charge of £7.50 per hour for research involved in postal enquiries.

Specialist sources, such as Blair Castle Archives, the Hornel Art Gallery & Library at Kircudbright, and the Clan Donald Centre on Skye make charges for research to cover their costs, and certain universities are now making charges for their services to outsiders.

As a rule, no other charges are levied, except for providing photocopies. As you get more detailed and accurate results from photocopies or printouts, you are best to say you will pay for copies of the relevant material. Quite a number of libraries and archives are now able to do printouts from microfilm holdings. Charges per page vary markedly. Give the library a cash limit for this, so they know how far they can take this. If you are fairly certain of the likely costs, include your cheque for the estimated amount. If you overestimate the charge, why not tell them to keep the change? You were willing to pay it, and it is still a bargain service - try any commercial genealogical researcher's charges!

The basic rule is: keep it simple, and keep it short, and you will get the best, fastest, and cheapest results.

When writing to countries outside the U.K., always enclose International Reply Coupons, available from main post offices, to cover likely postage costs back to you.

Most university libraries will be helpful provided a) you are doing research which really requires their facilities and b) you come when they are not busy with their own readers. It is best to enquire beforehand to see when you should call, and check on possible charges. Remember that public enquiries are a helpful extra, not a right that you have.

Archives should also be considered in their own context. They are there primarily to preserve records as an historical source, and they do not have genealogy as their main interest. Many of them quite willingly do much for family historians, but they must have care for the often unique records in their care, and may impose restrictions on use. Observe these meticulously. Your actions towards these archives may influence their future availability to other family historians.

The same applies to national archives such as the Scottish Record Office. Observe the rules with care, as they are not imposed frivolously. They protect irreplaceable historical records which are invaluable as a national resource.

In addition, should you come (or write in) with a particular document in mind, try to clearly identify the document in advance, preferably by quoting its reference number if given in published works. This saves the staff, and yourself, time and effort.

ENQUIRIES ELSEWHERE

Within the U.K., you can send enquiries to places like the Public Record Office in England or New Register House in Edinburgh, but they will charge for making a search for an entry in the census. You may also use a paid researcher, at your own risk. Standards are not easily guaranteed in this field, and often a dedicated and careful amateur is just as good, particularly if you can get a printout of the census page, so avoiding copying errors.

If you are a member of a family history society in a distant area or country, often one of the other members will be willing to look up a census entry for you, provided you give enough detail to make identification fairly easy. The society may perhaps offer an organised search facility utilising its own members' geographical propinquity to suitable sources of census data. Treat such facilities as you would a library - keep your enquiry clear and simple!

However, if you can get to where the microfilm is, that is the best solution : you can talk over your query with a member of the local library staff, who may help you by telling you that the village you want is not on the reel you thought it would be, because of boundary changes. They may also have additional sources about the village, or even the family, that you would otherwise not have encountered. A postal query can only ask limited questions, and will probably receive only the answer asked for, and nothing extra, due to staff shortage.

BASIC PROBLEMS WITH THE CENSUS RETURNS

A small number of 1841 returns have not survived, so in these cases you can only start with 1851. A few losses have also occurred in 1881 and 1891 material. The missing returns, according to the Registrar General in Edinburgh, are:

1841- Fife parishes of Abdie, Auchtermuchty, Balmerino, Ceres, Collessie, Creich, Cults, Cupar, Dairsie, Dunbog, Kinghorn, Kinglassie, Kirkcaldy, Leslie, and Auchinleck in Ayrshire.

1881 - parish of Dunscore, and enumeration books nos.13-27 are missing from the Dumfries returns.

1891 - enumeration book no.4 is missing from the Kelso returns.

I also understand that book 8 is missing from the 1861 returns for Methven, Perthshire.

The 1841 census, although it gives the names of all the people in a family, leaves much to be desired from the viewpoint of the family historian. First of all, the relationship to the head of the family is not stated, so a couple could be man and wife or brother and sister. An elderly person could be an aunt or mother or a sick neighbour - the census simply lists those in the house on census night. Fortunately, from 1851 the relationship is asked for and usually given.

The next problem is an individual's birthplace. In 1841 the enumeration schedule simply asked whether you were born in the county, or not. The answer was put down as Y for yes or N for no, with an initial if born in another country (E for England, I for Ireland, etc.)

You will find the same arrangement in reverse in England, where a Scottish birthplace in 1841 just states "S" for Scotland, with similar exceptions to the rule.

The "Yes" answers were so numerous that often a tick in the column was all that was done by the enumerator. It was a silly question, and from 1851 the schedule asked for the parish of birth, if in Scotland, and giving only the country for outside Scotland, although I have noticed an English birthplace not uncommonly appear as London, instead of England. Even more unusual, in one Dundee example the birthplace column records one person as born "Blackfriar's Rd., London" You can't get much luckier than that! Irish birthplaces are usually just Ireland, though again I have found "County Cavan, Ireland" and even "Monaghan", omitting the fact that this is a county in Ireland.

Although foreign countries are supposed to be simply an initial letter, often you find more detail, such as West Indies, or Jamaica, or Bengal. Foreign births are very common in the families of military men or seamen who may have married overseas or had children born overseas. You will also find failed colonists or fortune-hunters who returned home with children born abroad. I have an ancestor like this who was born in Australia while his parents were at the gold fields, but the family returned to Scotland a few years later.

Foreigners who normally lived abroad may be found in Scotland aboard ships in harbour, working in specialised occupations (e.g. dancing master), held in prison, or serving in the British forces - many Irishmen served in Scotland, such as the Aberdeen barracks in the 1851 census.

CHECKING THE FACTS

A word of warning here, regarding birthplaces. Normally the head of the household answered the questions and wrote the answers, or the enumerator did in the frequent cases of illiteracy. This means that one person may be filling in what he THINKS are the correct answers, without checking his facts.

Someone whose family moved from Aberdeen to Dundee when he was a baby may have grown up in Dundee and think that Dundee was his birthplace. He will give Dundee as the answer, leaving you with a problem in finding his birth. Conversely, you may have the luck to find an exact village of birth, instead of the parish, or even, in one case, where the place of birth is down as "Fort George", which is the military barracks near Inverness. Probably the worst birthplace of all is "at sea", if no explanatory information is added.

The real solution to dubious birthplaces, as in other situations in family history, is to extend your research to find corroborative material. Check all the censuses you can for the same family. Your relative who earlier did not know his birthplace - you find "N.K." entered as Not Known - may have later known the correct answer, or a brother or sister may be with them at a census and give the correct place of birth. Even memories can fail. One lady born in Fraserburgh married in Craig parish, Montrose, and lived many years there until in one census her place of birth appears as Craig parish, the same as all the rest of the family. She was now accepted as a native, it seems! Fortunately the other censuses say Fraserburgh.

Another reason for checking every census for the same family is that you occasionally find relatives staying with them. Best of all are elderly folk. This can get you back two generations at one blow.

For example, I found an Alexander Mitchell, age 89, living with his 50-year-old grandson and family in

Glasgow in 1861. His place of birth was Paisley. Being 89, he didn't have long to live and escape me again. I found his death recorded at the end of 1861, giving me his parents, whose marriage I soon found in 1758, in Paisley Abbey parish, so I had gained 100 years by that piece of luck in the 1861 census.

The next matter of importance is ages. First of all, take great care with the 1841 census ages. You will find that most are multiples of 5; e.g. 25, or 30, or 35. The reason was that for statistical reasons, people were to be grouped in 5-year bands for ages, and the schedule asked for ages of everyone 15 or over to be rounded down to the nearest 5th year. This was not an easy concept for most folk, and often you will find the correct age given, but mostly they are in the rounded down form. This means that anyone who is listed as 50 may be any age from 50 to 54, and you have to take that into account when estimating a date of birth.

For children the correct age was expected, but inevitably some folk didn't get the idea properly, and you may find more than one child listed as 10 and 15. They are not necessarily twins or triplets!

Go on to 1851 and check the ages there, for more exact information. Even here, you will probably find that a person does not always age by ten years between the censuses. The reasons are several. First, the technical one. Because of the variation in the census dates, someone born in the April-May period will quite correctly be one year different from the ten-year gap. Allow for a year either side, in every case where you do not know the month of birth - which is most times.

The second, simpler reason for age variation is this - if I ask you your age, will you tell me the truth? You may have been born before your parents married, or you may have told your husband you were a couple of years younger than you really were when you met and married (and he is the one filling in the form), or you may not be able to get a sensible answer out of great-auntie Flo who is visiting you, so you put down your best guess.

There are hundreds of reasons why an age will be put down wrongly, despite the strictures against telling lies on the form. If the subject interests you, there was an article by J.C.Dunlop -"Misstatement of age on the returns of the Census of Scotland" in the Journal of the Royal Statistical Society, vol.86 (1923).

That's once again why corroboration is needed. Check all available sources, from marriage certificates and death certificates to seaman's or other trade documents - anything which gives an age. You can't always blame the I.G.I. for something not being found where you expect it to be!

CLARIFYING THE FACTS

Of course, you can use the census data in the reverse way, noting the appearance of an individual each decade until he disappears, and that gives you a ten year period for his possible death or move to a new address. A death usually leaves the rest of the family at the same address. Identify the death certificate and it should then lead you to further information, perhaps even a new address at which to find more family members.

The data given under the heading Rank, Profession or Occupation usually appears in a standard set of titles decided upon by the census people. All girls and women, for example, who did not have outside employment, and so helped out at home, were listed as Domestic Servant or Family Servant. Independent meant someone of independent means who did not have to work for a living. Annuitant meant someone in receipt of a pension of some kind.

Social status was important at the time. Anyone who was in receipt of poor relief had their entry put in as Pauper, while owners of businesses or farms had to add details of number of employees, and no. of acres if a farm - a particularly helpful extra.

Children at school were described as Scholar, and from the ages of those who are so marked, you can tell something about the level of local education. University graduates normally gave their university as well as the degree. Some occupations given in the census may differ from that on, say, a marriage certificate, because the enumerator would select from a standard list of occupations rather than use an individual's own, perhaps more descriptive, occupational title. The standard list lends itself better to statistical analysis of the returns.

CENSUS BOOKS - THE LAYOUT IS GEOGRAPHIC

We must not neglect the way the census documentation is organised if we are to get the most information from it. Most importantly, everything is arranged geographically, by the address. Each document is an enumeration book, and at the start of each book is a statement of the geographical area included. Normally a group of enumeration books will together cover a parish, but in big towns and cities the enumeration areas may not fit the parish boundaries.

For cities there are street name indexes, which will direct you to the books for particular streets and even house numbers. Microfilm of certain census returns may include a street index, as in the case of Dundee. The smaller places have no indexes at all, except where family history societies and individuals have indexed them. Some street indexes have been compiled locally, such as the ones for Paisley and Greenock.

So in order to find your relatives quickly, you need an address, preferably a street, but in country parishes the village will be all you get - most village streets were not named until late on last century. After all, a'body kent a'body in the village! Major movements in village population are a modern phenomenon.

Where do you get your addresses?

Here are some ideas for places to look, which you can find at home or in libraries and archives: Birth, marriage, and death certificates, baptismal certificates,wills and testaments, lair documents for family graves; school records; occupational documents, from indentures to professional memberships; society and club affiliation (Masonic certificates, etc.); taxation records (Cess books, valuation rolls), property records (register of sasines) and other legal documents. Newspapers are very useful for trade notices, obituaries, and major events such as accidents. Graveyard burial registers and monumental inscriptions can be surprisingly informative - a house name or sometimes street address may be given.

Trade and Post Office directories were produced for all the major towns and cities but not very many have survived in local libraries for the very early years. These usually include the head of the household, and a trade address may also refer to a private address elsewhere. To find data on most smaller burghs and villages, check in the County Directories, although some of the smaller places have directories too - for example Strathkelvin Libraries have Bishopbriggs directories from 1848 and voters' rolls of Kirkintilloch from 1839.

More personal sources may be letters and diaries or family scrapbooks, which you may find in the possession of other members of the family. An elderly relative may be willing to dip into her private diary to tell you her great-aunt's address at the turn of the century, which may be the same one where the family stayed way back in 1881 if you are lucky. The fly-leaves of books, particularly bibles and other religious works, and school prizes, can be rich sources of names and addresses.

If you are really unlucky, you'll encounter the problem I have had. Some of my ancestors lived for decades in Glasgow, but moved so often that pinning them down for a census was most frustrating. I would find a marriage certificate with addresses, but neither party was found there at the census before or after that year. Each child would be born at a different address, and even where the family appeared in a census, someone would be missing from the home.

The problem is acute in urban areas, but less intractable in smaller communities, where a search around the rest of the community often turns up the family.

If you have to do this, confirm that it is the same family by checking the parents' and children's names and ages against your earlier information. It is not unknown for two couples with identical names to be having children in the same community, but they are less likely to be of similar ages or use the same naming of children.

MISSING PERSONS

For explanation of some of the persons missing from a census, it is worth examining the enumerator's report in each enumeration book. He will often include notes to explain his failure to achieve a complete return.
The note may conversely explain the appearance of strangers in the return, perhaps working on a new harbour or railway project.

In the earlier censuses, up to 1831, military personnel were not recorded, and although they were supposed to be included from 1841 onwards, the enumerator may have wrongly assumed that the previous policy still stood. Fortunately muster rolls and other military lists can fill this gap.

Another cause of omission lies in the fact that the enumeration books, which you see now, were compiled from the original schedules used at the actual households. These originals were later destroyed, so we are unable to determine which information was filled in by the householder, and which by the enumerator. During transcripion an entire family might be lost, although the enumeration numbering was designed to prevent this sort of thing. A mislaid return could appear as an uninhabited house. The enumerator may have misread the original handwriting, or "corrected" apparent errors, turning the family surname into a new one. He may even have filled in gaps on the basis of guesswork or local knowledge for the sake of completeness. There is no way of knowing whether and how often this happened.

Fishermen are often omitted from the census, particularly the earlier ones. Later they were entered at the first port of call, if within a day or two. Earlier, the enumerator would simply record that about twenty fishermen were absent on the night of the census, and that is all you will find. Seafaring men on board ships sailing in Scottish waters were recorded in the later censuses in two ways. Men on Royal Navy vessels were enumerated and the returns sent to the census office by the Admiralty; merchant marine sailors were recorded similarly through the Registrar-General of shipping and seamen, London.

A special schedule was prepared for use by the shipping population. It provided spaces for the place the schedule was delivered to the Master, the position of the vessel at midnight on Census Day, and the number of persons who were on shore on the night of the census. The customs officers at the ports filled in the sections on the port to which the ship belonged, tonnage, whether steam or sailing vessel, and usage at the time. The schedules were then sent to the Registrar General for shipping in London, who then forwarded them to the appropriate national Registrar General. You can expect to find them with the census returns for the port.

Practice regarding ships varied over the census years, with initially only ships in port being recorded, later with ships recorded at their first UK port of call within a very short period. Vessels outside UK territorial waters are ignored, unless they are Royal Navy vessels, which enumerated its complement on census day wherever they happened to be in the world. The records are then held by the vessel name.

For ships berthed in a harbour, the standard enumeration book may be utilised, with the vessel's home port placed in the address column. Passengers as well as crew are included in the return. Although some of the persons on board ship may be related, the relationship column in examples I have examined has not been completed. The occupation column may include details such as "emigrant" for a passenger about to leave home for ever.

Locating Scots on board ship can mean checks on ships in harbours all over the UK, as the seaborne population last century was quite large and far-travelled. Some Scots noted in harbour at Stepney, London, in 1871 were on board a schooner, the Victoria, of 180 tons, crewed entirely by Aberdonians, mostly young unmarried men.

Returning to solid ground, enumerators were supposed to record only those present at an address, but I spotted an entry for the head of a household, fully completed, but with an extra entry "(absent)"!!! Another schedule pointed out to me by a researcher had a pencilled note "family are away" after the entry for the head of household.

Although not available to researchers for many years to come, 1921 was particularly bad for people not being where they should be. The reason was that the 1921 census was taken in June, when many people were on holiday. This was particularly noticeable in the apparent sharp increase in population in places like Argyll and Bute, due to the presence of holidaymakers.

Anyone travelling around the country, say overnight by train, would be entered at the address they arrived at in the morning. That could be a hotel, lodging house, army barracks, or similar establishments. Some people are away from home by the nature of their work, e.g. a shepherd may be out on the hills, and might not be recorded at all.

More permanent absences would be people in hospital or insane asylum, in prison, or in the armed services. Some paupers may be found in the workhouse, other folk may be in their place of employment such as a ship in harbour, a hotel, boarding school, hospital, or army barracks. Many teenage girls were employed in domestic service in other folks houses, even in very poor communities.

People in institutions were not always recorded as fully as they should have been, particularly in prisons, where sometimes only the surname and first initial is given, or even worse, only two initials and no full name at all. It is worth remembering that some people may be in jail not for any real crime, but because they are in debt.

In cases of army barracks, treated as an Institution, the ranking officers are listed before the other ranks. The spouse and family are normally listed immediately after the soldier, which helps identification. In the case of Aberdeen Barracks in 1851, relationships are added in the occupations column of the Institutions enumeration book, e.g. "Son of J.Brand", and even more helpfully, for soldiers who were almost all Irish, the Irish County and parish of birth are given throughout, instead of the official injunction to be listed as "I" for Ireland only. In the family of the Officer Commanding, the children are all born in different places and in various parts of the world, reflecting his postings over the years.

Other people are missing for their own reasons, either because they were criminals or thought they were wanted for some sort of misdemeanour. They may have changed their name, which is entirely legal in Scotland just by telling people that you want to be known by that name from now on; there is no legal formality such as England has. Alternatively, there may be some family or personal reason why they do not wish to reveal their true name. These can be problems, but normally the other members of the family will be there, and by a process of elimination you can make a reliable identification.

Beware of cases of second marriages. Where you find children in a family, of an age that implies the wife (the supposed mother) bore them at age 16 or less, you may reasonably suspect that she is a second wife, the first having died. (Divorce was uncommon in those days.)

It can be even more confusing if a couple marry and appear in the census as a family, but both have children by a previous marriage. Then you will perhaps find a mixture of surnames for the children, but perhaps all listed under one surname, with some referred to as step-children in the relationship column. How it appears depends on how the family reported themselves on the form.

As always, check the census before and after, to see if you can confirm your suspicions. If the children's ages suggest a possible date of marriage, and it is after 1854, try to locate the marriage certificate, which should identify the parties as widowed or not. The woman's name would give her former married surname, with her parents' names revealing her maiden surname. You can then, from the ages of the children of the former

29

marriage deduce a likely period for the first marriage, and get a step further along that road.

A point worth mentioning is the occasional appearance of women under their maiden name. This sometimes happens in rural areas of Scotland where a married woman still used her maiden surname in the village. The official requirement was to enter a women under her married surname, but lapses did occur, particularly if she is the first person on a new page.

One lapse I spotted was where a wife's maiden name had been inserted, then crossed out, being replaced with the standard "Do". It occurred even more with widows, who would state their name using their original surname, and the enumerator would have no way of knowing this was not a married name if there was no family with a different surname at the address. Often though, you find a woman listed as widow, and children of hers with a different surname. You have then a very good chance of identifying her deceased husband from that surname.

Name variations can appear, however, on a more personal basis, that of an individual's preference. For example, someone may be known popularly by one name, but his or her officially recorded name may be something else. My own daughter's name is Alexandra Young Johnson, but at school she picked up a nickname, which she has kept using, and to most people nowadays her first name is Zak. She could give that name at the next census, and so it would be shown, although there is no evidence of that name in other records.

Difficulties over names can include a misreading of the abbreviated name "Margt." as "Mary", due to poor writing or faded ink. Other names may suffer from the same problem. In addition, there are many variants of popular names, so that Tibby equals Elizabeth, and Charnock equals Charlotte. Watch out for the local variations.

Such differences in name can cause confusion. I have another similar problem in my own family history. One great-uncle started off as an operatic singer, and adopted a stage name, Arthur Lynn. We even have old gramophone records he made later, when he went off to the U.S.A. and turned evangelist, singing a new tune! He kept to his stage name, and now I don't know whether he married using the name Arthur Lynn, or his real name, David Brown Johnson. The family lost touch with him, and as he moved around, I don't even know which state he married in, or when. He died in Florida in 1945.

Genealogy can be frustrating, when people are awkward like this! My fishing forebears were simple folk, staying in the same village and behaving themselves, ...as a rule. It's my Johnsons who won't stay still, even if they stay in Glasgow all their lives. They kept moving house. Roll on the day when we get a comprehensive index to the Censuses, probably computerised and stored on CD-ROM discs!

Folk who move around can sometimes be better identified through a census than any other document. Take this one, from Peebleshire in 1861: (abbreviated)

NAME & AGE	OCCUPATION	PLACE OF BIRTH
Thomas Gray,56	Minister	Aberdeen
Harriet Gray,wife,36		Ionian Islands
George Gray,son,10		Edinburgh
John Fraser,unmarr.,46	Gardener	Morayshire,Duthill

There is enough in the birthplaces to link together a number of far-flung places for one family, and perhaps explain why Harriet's birth certificate was so hard to find! Another curious point in the entry is that Duthill is in Inverness-shire, not Morayshire!

Some names can be difficult to find because they have been spelled differently. An enumerator may put down a name spelled the way it sounded to him, and not the way you use it today. So if you don't spot your family name, go back through the book and watch out for a surname that sounds the same, then check the members of the family to see if they fit the pattern you should expect to find, in forenames and ages.

Watch out for the problem of misleading description - a person may be listed as "relative" or "servant" or "visitor" when they might more properly be described as Cousin or Aunt or such. When you take notes, record EVERY person in the household, not just the ones you recognise as related. The data may make sense only years later. An "employee" in the household may turn out to be the wife's cousin brought into the family business.

POINTS TO REMEMBER

When you read through the page of the census, remember these points:

1. The family may continue over the page!

2. The household may be one of several in the building. This is indicated by short lines drawn below the last member of the household. As a variety of markings were used, I'll not try to explain them in detail, but they should be fairly evident when you watch for them. The standard markings are one short line at the end of the family group (the household), and two short lines at the end of the building's occupants. All other marks can usually be ignored; various scorings or ticks were the action of staff making counts for the statistics.

3. The number in the first column on the left is the enumeration number, not the house number. This is an easy mistake to make, as many streets did not have a house number at the time of the census.

4. Check on the families on the same pages and the ones before and after - there may be relatives in the vicinity.

5. Take note of additional information, such as number of rooms with windows. This gives you some indication of the living conditions of the family.

6. Another useful piece of information to be found in the census return is whether a person is deaf, dumb, or blind, and in the 1871 census there was added also whether a person was an imbecile, idiot, or lunatic. If for example you don't find a person at home at some censuses, and later find him at home, noted as a lunatic, his absence previously may mean that he was in an institution, and you will have another source to check.

7. If your family seems to be missing, go back to the start of the enumeration book. There will be a description of the area covered by this book, and you may find that the other side of the street, or further along the same street, where your family may live, is in another book. Another possibility is that the street name was changed between censuses. Check the street index for this possibility, if you are dealing with a city. Local directories, arranged by street, can give valuable clues to variations in street names.

8. You will find extra children in the 1851 census in Scotland, who are not found in the OPR indexes or IGI. The reason for this is the 1843 crisis in the Church of Scotland when the breakaway congregations formed the Free Church of Scotland. Many of the Church of Scotland ministers then refused to register children baptised in the Free Church, and as that was anything up to three-quarters of the local population, it means many children are not in the registers. The 1851 census finds them, if still living, and from the ages you can pin down their birth to within a year or so.

FINDING YOUR PLACE - INDEXES OF VARIOUS KINDS

Place names often were altered over the years, particularly farms and cottages, and new streets appeared in the census as building progressed. Place name indexes are therefore very useful in locating your relatives. Of course, it can be surprising when an American or Canadian tells you that the ancestral farm was near the city of Rhynie, which is a tiny village!

Various census reports have included place-name indexes or they were published separately. One appears for the 1831 census at the end of volume 2 (H.M.S.O.,1833). For 1841, there was an index for Scotland, published in 1843[1841 census - Index to names of places, Scotland. H.M.S.O.,1843]. The 1851 census - Index to Names of Places in the Population Tables(H.M.S.O.,1852) covered the whole UK in one volume. There was a general index for Scotland in volume 2 of the 1881 census report(H.M.S.O.,1833). The same happened for the 1891 census.

Place-name indexes are later less frequent, with England & Wales being better served than Scotland. "Place-names and population for Scotland" (H.M.S.O.,1967) can still prove a useful guide for identification of farms and estates, and even small hamlets, if you are unsure of the location of the place-name.

Registration districts were normally parishes, but not always so. In cities, the parish or the civil registration district contained thousands of people, and thus smaller geographical units were needed to be fair to the enumerators. These were the enumeration districts, usually one E.D. per book. You will find that while a country area of huge size may be covered by half a dozen enumeration districts, the city enumeration district was only a few streets in a densely populated area. These districts were not arranged in logical order, so you cannot assume that the continuation of a street is found in the next book in numerical order.

A guide, for England and Wales only, is "Index to Census Registration Districts" by Bryant, Rosier & Marfleet, (Federation of Family History Societies, Birmingham, 1986). The confusion about these districts is got over by having street indexes for the big cities, and these exist for each census. They direct you to the correct enumeration book for each street or part of a street.

Moving from place indexes to person indexes, the Federation of Family History Societies has produced a fourth edition (1992) of its "Marriage, Census and other Indexes for family historians". The Society of

Genealogists has also a 1988 edition of its booklet "Census Indexes in the library of the Society of Genealogists". Very few Scottish indexes are in this, only about eight items, compared to seven pages of indexes for Lincolnshire.

Scottish census indexes are most easily found by checking the library additions for each of the local family history societies. For example, the April 1988 newsletter of the Glasgow & West of Scotland society gives among its list of library additions: 1851 census indexes for Rosneath, Arrochar, and Luss, all in Dunbartonshire. These are actually more than indexes, as full census data is attached to each name in this alphabetical listing. The same additions list includes a street index for Kirkcaldy, and one for Dysart, 1861 census, produced by the Fife Local Studies Workshop - it is not just genealogists that produce helpful indexes.

Some indexes have been published in unusual places. The Clackmannan County 1841 Census Index has been published in Utah, USA(ed. by R.V.Jackson et al.). The persons named in full in this index are heads of households and anyone living in the household who has a different surname.

The Glasgow and West of Scotland F.H.S. has been indexing the 1851 Glasgow census, and this mammoth task has been helped by using computers. By the end of 1990 the Glasgow City area had been completed, covering 156,783 names. Barony, the sprawling civil parish round Glasgow City, was still being indexed by spring, 1991, with only Shettleston completed of the 8 civil parishes within Barony. Bridgeton and Calton were due next. Searches can be made of this database, for a large s.a.e. and a donation based on the number of names to be searched for. Contact the society for further details.

Dundee City Libraries now have a name index to the 1841 census of Dundee, entirely the work of one man, William Binnie.

Hamilton District libraries have compiled a place/street index to the 1841-1881 returns for their area, as a local aid. Renfrew District Museums and Art Galleries Service have compiled a street index for Paisley and Abbey parishes, 1841-1881, and volunteers have recently indexed the Greenock parishes for them, covering 1841 and 1851. Their enthusiasm is such that it is safe to say that other parishes will be indexed by the Paisley Volunteers before too long. If only other authorities were so lucky, or keen to foster such programmes!

East Kilbride Central Library has a surname index to the 1881 census for East Kilbride parish, and they have a place-name index (1841-91) in preparation.

The William Coull Anderson Library of Genealogy at Arbroath has a typescript indexed copy of the 1851 census for Carmyllie.

Moray District Libraries have various surname indexes for St. Andrews-Lhanbryde (1841), Birnie (1841-1881), & Aberlour, Banff, Boyndie, Fordyce, Gamrie, Marnoch, Mortlach, Ordiquhill, Rathven, and Rothiemay (all 1851).

Dumbarton Library has a variety of census indexes for the Dumbarton area, including one for all McGregors in Dunbartonshire, 1851.

Indexes are invaluable, for as you remember, all entries are by place. Any indexing is welcome, but the better it is done, the more accurate and therefore useful it will be. I tried my hand at this with the 1841 census of Craig parish, Montrose, and produced a surname index. This merely tells you which page of which enumeration books for the parish contain entries with that surname.

However, if the index could be of individuals, then all the better. Imagine the task, though. It is the sort of thing only a group could contemplate on any large scale, and many of the English societies have embarked on these. It is a major project that requires dedication on the scale of graveyard recording, but has the advantage of being an indoor job.

One lady, Margaret Shand, in Queensland, Australia, has done some sterling and lonely work in transcribing and indexing the Banffshire parishes for 1851. The Aberdeen F.H. Society intends to publish these when complete, giving us all a further reference tool for searches. Apart from those already mentioned, the Aberdeen society holds indexes for Midmar (1841,1851); and Echt (1851).

The Highland Family History Society has published indexes to the 1851 census for the parishes of Kiltearn, Kincardine (with Croick), Knockbain, Tain, Wick, and Killearnan.

A major indexing project for the 1881 census in England, Wales, Isle of Man and Channel Islands has been going on since 1988, under the auspices of the Mormon Church and the British Genealogical Record Users Committee. The indexes, on microfiche, are appearing gradually for each county. There are several different indexes using the same data, such as a Surname Index, Birthplace Index, Notes Index, a List of Institutions, and List of vessels/ships by name.

A similar project for indexing Scotland's 1881 census has now been started, with the cooperation of the Scottish Association of Family History Societies, the General Register Office for Scotland, and the Genealogical Society of Utah (Mormons), but will take much longer to complete.
The process involves volunteers transcribing, from photocopies, the material in the census, to make it

easily read for input into a computer database. The database is then used to produce the indexes required.

PARISH AND COUNTY

Another confusion in census searching lies in whether a parish is in one county or another. How can you get a parish to be in two different counties at the same time? The answer is that some parishes actually straddle the county boundary, and for census purposes the enumerators were instructed to regard a parish as being in the county in which its greater part lay.

The result was that your ancestor may have lived all his life in a village which was always in, say Banffshire, but if the majority of the census enumeration area lay in Aberdeenshire then the census records for the whole parish were recorded as being Aberdeenshire.

Other examples are: Alva parish, which was in Stirlingshire, but after 1891 moved to Clackmannanshire. Logie parish moved from Perthshire to Stirlingshire. Coupar Angus was in Perthshire, then became part of Forfarshire, which became Angus County.

A similar problem exists where an entire chunk of countryside is in one county, but completely detached from the rest of the county. This occurs in the north-east, where parts of Banffshire existed for many years as enclaves within Aberdeenshire. They are now officially Aberdeenshire, but at the time of your research, census or anything else, the family that stayed in the one place may have correctly been in Banffshire.

You may be confused at some of the birthplace entries for individuals. Errors were common, where neither the person nor the enumerator was familiar with non-local parishes. Often the county given for a parish is wrong, or even non-existent, such as Edinburgh-shire instead of Midlothian. Kincardineshire often appears as Mearns, and when people were unsure of the parish, then simply the county would be recorded.

However, sometimes errors can work in your favour. Only in the local County are you supposed to get the local placename, but just the county for elsewhere in Scotland, and the country name for elsewhere.
Here is an abbreviated example from East Lothian, Tranent parish, 1861, with my * indicating birthplace wrongly entered but helpful:

NAME & AGE	OCCUPATION	PLACE OF BIRTH
William Marr, 48	gatekeeper & Chelsea Pensioner	County of Aberdeen
Ellen Marr,wife,38		Manchester*
Elizabeth Marr,dau.,19	dressmaker	Ireland,Dublin*
Alexander Marr,son,13	scholar	Malta
Ellen Marr,daughter,9		Inverness,Fort George*

SCOTLAND.

ENUMERATOR'S SCHEDULE.

County of _Aberdeen_

District of _Deer_

Parish of _Fraserburgh_

City of

Burgh Royal and Parliamentary of

Burgh Parliamentary (not being Royal) of

Burgh and Parish of

Island of

No. of Enumeration District _One_

Description of ditto _So much of the Parish of Fraser-_
-burgh as lies between the sea and East side
of Broad street inclusive with Lighthouse
at Kinairds Head being part of the Borough
of Regality of Fraserburgh.

B 1

4G

CENSUS. SCOTLAND.

County of *Aberdeen*

Parish of *Ellon*

_____ May, 1841.

We the undersigned hereby agree to act as Enumerators for the Parish
of _____ *Ellon* _____ for the purpose of
taking the Census, on Monday the 7th of June, and the following days, under the
superintendence of the Person appointed by the Sheriff as Divider of the Parish.

SIGNATURES OF ENUMERATORS.

Wm Chalmers
Geo Mackie
John Riddel

George Bowman
Alexr Egerton
George Edward
John Edward
W Hay (in room of Mr. Riddell)
Thos Shirreffs
James Miller
Geo Clark
Wm Lillie

22

City of _____

Burgh of _____

Parish of _____

Village of _____

After the completion of the Enumeration, and before this Schedule is delivered to the person appointed by the Sheriff or Provost for revision, the Enumerator is requested to fill up the following Table as correctly as he can, according to such information as he can obtain, and to the best of his knowledge and belief.

	MALES.	FEMALES.	TOTAL.
Computed Number of persons who may have slept, in barges, boats, or other small vessels remaining stationary on canals or other inland navigable waters			
Or in mines or pits			
Or in Tents or in the open air			
Or in barns, sheds, or otherwise, and have not been enumerated in the Schedule, although abiding in the District on the night of the 6th of June			
			Total.

Remarks of Schoolmaster or other Person appointed to divide the Parish by the Sheriff or Provost, which apply to all the six Enumeration Districts of the Parish of Aberlemno.

On examining the Enumeration Schedules for the Parish of Aberlemno, I find, that the numbers stated in the Columns "Inhabited Houses" refer to the "distinct Families"; but as there are 7 Houses in the Parish containing each 2 families & one containing 3 families — the total number of Distinct families in the Parish, is 221, whilst the total number of Inhabited Houses is only 212.

In this enumeration of Inhabited Houses, the Bothies (or out-houses for servants) of which, there are 22 in the Parish; are each considered as a separate Inhabited house.

The term Crofter as applied in the Schedules, refers to such persons as rent about 4, 6, 8, 10 &c. acres of land, but in no case except one, amounting to 20 acres; such individuals, it will be seen, generally follow some other avocation.

All the Weavers are Hand-Loom, and the material flax, without exception.

The decrease of Population in this Parish since 1831 is accounted for, from the circumstance, — that the pavement-Quarries on the Estates of Tillywhandland & Flemington in the Parish, which employed from 20 to 30 men, have not been wrought for several years — also a quarry on the Estate of Carse, which employed about 20 men, was not wrought during last year — & a flax-spinning Mill, on a small scale, at Blackiemill, which employed from 30 to 40, was also given up some years ago. —

I have got notice of one man only, who has left this Parish within the last six months for a foreign country Viz Australia.

1841: REMARKS OF THE SCHOOLMASTER, PARISH OF ABERLEMNO, ANGUS. THIS CAN GIVE, AS HERE, USEFUL EXTRA INFORMATION ABOUT THE POPULATION NOT RECORDED IN THE MAIN BODY OF THE ENUMERATION BOOKS.

(reproduced by permission of HMSO)

Parish of *Fraserburgh*

1

1			2			3	4	
PLACE	HOUSES		NAME and SURNAME, SEX and AGE, of each Person who abode in each House on the Night of 6th June.			OCCUPATION	WHERE BORN	
Place, Name of Village, Street, Square, Close, Court, &c.	Uninhabited or Building	Inhabited	NAME and SURNAME	AGE Male	AGE Female	Of what Profession, Trade, Employment, or whether of Independent Means.	If Born in Scotland, state whether in County or otherwise	Whether Foreigner, or whether Born in Ireland
Broad Street		1	William Johnston	55		Army P.	Y	
			Jannet do.		55		Y.	
			William do.	20		Cooper J.		B.
			Barbra do.		15		Y.	
			Barbra Ironside		6		Y.	
			Giulina do		5		Y.	
Do.		1	Elizabeth Otterbank		50	Publican	Y.	
			Sarah do.		7		Y	
			Charlotte do.		10		Y	
			John Chalmers	20		Shoemaker	Y	
			Mary do.		15	F. S.	Y	
			Jean do.		15	F. S.	Y	
			Ann Sim		70	Ind.	Y	
			Alexander Scott	50		Musician	Y.	
Do.		1	Alexander Sutherland	35		Mes. at Arms	No	1
			Forbes do.		25		Y	
			Margaret do.		8		Y.	
			Jessy do		6		Y.	
			Alexander do	5			Y.	
			Forbes do	4			Y.	
			Agnes do		3		Y.	
			Charles do	4 m.			Y.	
			Margaret Duthie		15	F. S.	Y.	
			Jessy Thornton		11	F. S.	Y.	
TOTAL in Page 1		3		7	17			

1841: A TYPICAL PAGE. NOTE THE ADULT AGES IN MULTIPLES OF 5, THE LACK OF RELATIONSHIPS, THE LACK OF STREET NUMBERS, AND THE UNINFORMATIVE BIRTH LOCATIONS.
(reproduced by permission of HMSO)

Name of the Institution ___ *Police Office*

NAMES of each Person who abode therein on the Night of Sunday, June 6th.	Age of Males.	Age of Females.	OCCUPATION, if any.	Whether Born in same County.	Whether Born in England, Ireland, or Foreign Parts.
John Rattery	45		Sergeant of Police	Yes	
Frances Milne	35		Night Patrole	N	
John MacKenzie	25		Watchman	No	
Charles Craig	30		do	N	
Robert Mills	40		do	N	
Peter Smart	25		do	Y	
James Donald	25		do	Y	
George Henderson	15		Vagrant Prisoner	N	
William Henderson	15		do	P	N
James MacDonald	15		do	P	N
David Parker	55		Men S.	P	N
			//		
TOTAL in Page 1 ..	//	/			

GENEALOGICAL SOCIETY
SALT LAKE CITY, UTAH AT:

NEW REGISTER HOUSE

EDINBURGH SCOTLAND

OPERATOR

H. WITHINGTON

DATE FILMED

17 JUL 1982

LIGHT METER SETTING

REDUCTION x

14

FILM EMULSION NUMBER

037/3233/04·06

FILM UNIT SER. NO.

64+2

D. 32|26

PROJECT NUMBER

SCTL 8 A

ROLL NUMBER

719

COUNTY

ABERDEEN

PARISH

FRASERBURGH

TITLE OF RECORD

CENSUS RETURNS

VOLUME/S

196

YEAR/S INCLUDED

1851

ITEM 2

1851: MICROFILMS START WITH A FULL TECHNICAL
DESCRIPTION. CHECK YOU HAVE THE RIGHT ONE, BEFORE
SEARCHING FURTHER.

(reproduced by permission of HMSO)

Estimated number of persons, who have *not been enumerated* as inmates of any dwelling house, but who it is believed have slept or abode in the District on the night preceding the day of Enumeration—

(b)

| | Persons | |
Males	Females	Total

In barges, boats, or other small vessels remaining stationary on canals or other navigable waters ......

In barns, sheds, or the like......

In tents, or in the open air......

The above numbers do not include people in coasting or other sea-going vessels, nor persons travelling on railways or otherwise, through the district

TOTAL ...

When *many persons* not inhabitants are present, or *many* of the settled inhabitants are temporarily absent :— The Enumerator must also return :

(c)

| Persons. | | |
Males.	Females.	Total.
60	20	80

(1) The *estimated number* of such persons who are returned in the subsequent pages as having slept in his district on the night of March 30th, but who were there only temporarily

(2) The *estimated number* of persons who were absent *from the district* on the night of March 30th, but who usually dwell in the district. ......

Seamen in ships, or in coasting vessels on the night of March 31st, should not be included in the estimate, as they will be returned at the ports.

[State here the cause of the absence of so many of the inhabitants, whether in fishing or in other employments.]

(d)

| Persons. | | |
Males.	Females.	Total.
4	12	16

---

is Book is delivered to the *Superintendent* of the Parish for revision, the *Enumerator* is required to fill up the following Tables as correctly as he can.

ENUMERATOR'S SUMMARY.

king this Summary, write in the line against the name of EACH *Parish* or *Quoad Sacra* Parish r of Houses and of their inmates ; and in a *second* line the computed numbers who were in the open air, from Table b. A *third* line must contain the total in the Parish or *Quoad Sacra* Parish, or in that part of the Parish or *Quoad Sacra* Parish Enumeration District; not, however, including the inmates of any Public Institution not d by him.

(a)

Name of each Parish or Quoad Sacra Parish, either wholly or partly in the Enumerator's District	Houses			Persons		
	Inhabited	Uninhabited	Building	Males	Females	Total
Parish [or Quoad Sacra Parish] of *Inverkeithing* Occupiers, Houses and Persons therein......... Persons not in Houses, from Table b.	236 145	1	1	521	625	1146
Total	236 145	1	1	521	625	1146
[The Summary to be continued if the Enumerator's District comprises parts of more than one Parish or Quoad Sacra Parish.]	145			521	625	1146
Total in the Enumeration District	236 145	1	1	521	625	1146

1851: ENUMERATOR'S SUMMARY: THIS CAN SOMETIMES PROVIDE NEW LINES OF ENQUIRY. HERE, THE PRESENCE OF EXTRA WORKMEN, AND THEIR DEPENDENTS, IS EXPLAINED AS THE BUILDING OF A HARBOUR.

(reproduced by permission of HMSO)

Parish of *Findhulsk*

Quoad Sacra Parish of

No. of House-holder's Schedule	Name of Street, Place, or Road, and Name or No. of House	Name and Surname of each Person who abode in the house, on the Night of the 30th March, 1851	Relation to Head of Family	Condition	Age of Males / Females	Rank, Profession, or Occupation	Where Born	Whether Blind, or Deaf-and-Dumb
5	Shore St. Carnago	Alexander Noble	Head	Mar	36	Fisherman	Aberdeen Findulage	
		Henry Jr.	Son				Do	
		Alexander Do	Son				Do	
		John Do	Son				Do	
		William Do	Son				Do	
		Elizabeth Do	Dau				Do	
6		Rebecca Inn	Dau			Having Act Knitting, Servant	Aberdeen Findulage	
		Mary Do	Dau				Do	
		Alexander Do	Son				Findulage	
		John Do	Son				Do	
7		Mary Burnett	Wife	Mar		Seaman's Wife	Aberdeen Findulage	
		Catherine Do	Dau				Do	
		Louis Do	Son				Do	
		Christina Do	Dau				Do	
8	Shore Street Carnago	Sophia Burnett	Wife	Mar	36		Aberdeen Pitskigo	
		Sophia Biddie	Step Dau				Do	
		Isabella Biddie	Step Dau				Do	
		Margaret S. Burnett	Dau				Do	

	Total of Houses		Total of Persons	
Total 1 2 U B	I			

Name of Street, Place, or Road, and Name or No. of House	Name and Surname of each Person who abode in the house, on the Night of the 30th March, 1851	Relation to Head of Family	Condition	Age of Male	Age of Female	Rank, Profession, or Occupation	Where Born	Whether Blind, or Deaf-and-Dumb
	Isabella Beverley	Wife	Mar		22	Engineer's Wife	Banffshire Portsoy	
	Alexander Beverley	Son		7 m			Aberdeenshire Ellon	
	Paul Gordon	Head	Mar	27		Mason	do Fyvie	
	Ann Gordon	Wife	Mar		26		do Old Rachlin	
	Elspet Gordon	dau	Wid		19	Farmer of	Banffshire	
	Caroline Gordon	dau	U		13	House servant	Portsoy	
	Elizabeth Macleod	dau			4	Scholar	do	
	James Smith	Head	Wid	42		Agricultural labourer	do	
	Margaret Smith	Wife	Mar		37		do	
	Hugh Milne	Head	Wid	42		Butcher	do Slains	
	Catherine Milne	dau	U		13		do Rathlin	
	Robert Bruce	son		13		Scholar	do Slains	
	Hugh Marwick	Head	Wid	33		Blacksmith Journeyman	Inverness-shire Cry	
	Elizabeth Cook	Wife	Mar		31		Morayshire	
	Hugh Jaffrey	grand Child		9		Scholar at home	Aberdeen	
	Alexander Bruce	do				do	do	
	Isabella Burnfgh	Wife	Mar		47	Shoemakers wife	do Fraser	
	Isabella Burnfgh	niece			9 m		do do	
	Betsy Cook	relation		6		Scholar	do Aberdeen	

Total of Houses: 10 A U A B 0 — Total of Persons: 7 W

1851: A MORE DESCRIPTIVE PAGE FOR OCCUPATIONS AND RELATIONSHIPS
(reproduced by permission of HMSO)

Parish of *Dunnet*

No. of House-holder's Schedule	Name of Street, Place, or Road, and Name or No. of House	Name and Surname of each Person who abode in the house, on the Night of the 30th March, 1861	Relation to Head of Family	Condition	Age of Male / Female	Rank, Profession, or Occupation	Where Born	Whether Blind, or Deaf-and-Dumb
85								
86								
87								
88								

Total of Persons

SUMMARY OF TOTALS IN THE FOLLOWING PAGES.

Page	No. of separate Occupiers	Houses Inhabited	Houses Uninhabited	Houses Building	Persons Male	Persons Female	Persons Total
29	179	7	7			45	215
30		3			7	16	15
31					10	14	15
32		2				11	20
33		4				11	15
34		5				11	20
35		2				11	20
36		2				11	16
37		1				5	20
38		2				9	20
39		4				7	14
40		4				11	20
41		2				11	20
42		2				11	20
43		3				9	17
44		4				11	20
45		6				9	20
46		4				11	20
47		3				11	21
48		4				9	18
49		2				11	20
50		3				13	20
51		4				11	20
52		2				13	20
53		2				9	17
54		2	2			13	20
55		4	1			10	20
56		4	3		10	10	20
	226	133	1	1	244	291	535

Page	No. of separate Occupiers	Houses Inhabited	Houses Uninhabited	Houses Building	Persons Male	Persons Female	Persons Total
57	226	133	7		244	291	535
58		3					20
59		3			5	6	19
60		2				11	20
61		1			2	13	20
62						11	20
63						11	20
64					13	11	20
65						5	20
66					7	11	20
67					7	11	20
68					7	12	18
69						11	20
70					6	9	15
71					6	14	20
72					8	11	19
73						11	20
74				1		5	20
75					12	12	20
76					5	12	17
77					6	12	20
78					5	13	18
79					7	11	18
80					7	14	20
81					6	5	15
82					14	4	18
83					7	12	17
84					10	10	20
TOTAL	226	133	1	1	485	589	1074

Houses / Persons (totals)

No. of separate Occupiers	Inhabited	Uninhabited	Building	Males	Females	Total
226	133	1	1	485	589	1074
236	145	1	1	521	625	1146
				521	625	1146

1851: STATISTICS SHOULD NOT BE IGNORED
(reproduced by permission of HMSO)

The undermentioned Houses are situate within the Boundaries of the

Civil Parish of _Nicholas_	Quoad Sacra Parish of _St Clements_	Police Burgh of	School Board District of _Aberdeen_	Parliamentary Burgh of _Aberdeen_	Town of	Parliamentary Division of _North Aberdeen_	Village or Hamlet of	Royal Burgh of _Aberdeen_	Island of
Municipal Burgh of _Aberdeen_			Burgh Ward of _St Clements_						

ROAD, STREET, &c., and No. or NAME of HOUSE	HOUSES			NAME and Surname of each Person	RELATION to Head of Family	CONDITION as to Marriage	AGE (last Birthday)		PROFESSION or OCCUPATION				WHERE BORN	Gaelic or G. & E.	Whether Deaf and Dumb, Blind, Lunatic, Imbecile, or Idiot
	Inhabited	Uninhabited or Building (B.)					Males	Females		Employer	Employed	Neither Employer nor Employed, but working on own account			
30 Albion St				Helen Wood	Wife	Mar.			Knitter				Montrose Forfarshire		
				Isabella do	Daur				do				Aberdeenshire Aberdeen		
				Barbara do	Daur				do				do		
				Jessie do	Daur								do		
16 & 20 do			1	Ann Keith	Head	W			Housekeeper				Aberdeenshire Aberdeen		2
				William Mill	Nephew				Fisherman				Aberdeenshire Peterhead		
				Robert do	Nephew	S			Fisherman do				do		
				Elizabeth do	Niece								do		
18 & 36 do			1	John Miller	Head	Mar.			Fishmaster (herring fisher)				Aberdeenshire Peterhead		2
				William do	Nephew			X	Fisherman				do		
				John do	son				Scholar				Aberdeenshire Aberdeen		
				Helen do	wife	Mar.							do		
				George do	son		X		Herring fisher boy				do		
14 & 36 do			1	James do	Head	Mar.		X	Marine Carpenter				Aberdeenshire Aberdeen		2
				Isabella do	wife	Mar.							do		
				Robert do	son				Scholar				do		
				Richard Fennick	Head			X	Fisherman				Aberdeenshire Peterhead		
				Norman do	son		3						do		
40 & 88 do			1	George do	son								do		2
				Annie Charles	Head	Mar.			Fisherman's wife (General Servant Domestic)		X		Aberdeenshire Aberdeen		
				William do	son				Fisherman				do		
				James do	son				do				do		
				Robert do	son				do				do		

| Total of Houses.... | 4 | — | | | | Total of Males and Females... | 12 | 13 | | | | | | | Total of Windowed Rooms, | 9 |

Note.—Draw the pen through such of the words of the headings as are inappropriate.

1891: NOTE THE NUMBER OF NON-SCOTS IN ABERDEEN!
(reproduced by permission of HMSO)

[Scot.—Sheet E.

The undermentioned Houses are situate within the Boundaries of the

Civil Parish of	Quoad Sacra Parish of	Police Burgh of	School Board District of	Burgh Ward of	Parliamentary Burgh of	Town of	Parliamentary Division of

ROAD, STREET, &c., and No. or NAME of HOUSE.	HOUSES			NAME and Surname of each Person.	RELATION to Head of Family.	CONDITION as to Marriage.	AGE (last Birthday)		PROFESSION or OCCUPATION.	Employer.	Employed.	Neither Employer nor Employed, but working on own account.	WHERE BORN.	Village or Hamlet of
	In-habited	Unin-habited (U.) or Building (B.)					Males	Females						

1891: OCCUPATIONS CAN LEAD TO OTHER SOURCE MATERIAL SUCH AS DIRECTORIES OF CLERGYMEN.

(reproduced by permission of HMSO)

Population of the Parish of
Balmaclellan
as collected Feb. 9th 1792.
by the Rev. James Thomson,
and published in the
Statistical Account of
Scotland,
by Sir John Sinclair, Bart.

Drumanister	Anthony Cunningham	50
	Isabel MacMillan	44
	Robt. Cunningham	13
	Andrew Cunningham	11
	Mary Cunningham	9
	William Cunningham	5
	James Cunningham	1½
	Elizabeth Cunningham	

Corridow,	Alexander Donaldson	50
	Margaret Raffel	50
	Elizabeth Donaldson	1
	John Macaw,	20
	James Macdill	15

Lochwie,	Robert Girmerie,	70
	Jane Main,	70
	Robert Girmerie,	35
	William Macaw,	12

Laggan.	James Gillespie,	66
	Agnes Ferguson,	59
	Isabel Ferguson	31

1792: A SURPRISINGLY CLEAR POPULATION LIST COMPLETE WITH AGES
(courtesy of Hornel Library & Art Gallery, Kirkcudbright)

Burgh Census. District from Cross to Barn-hill. North Side of Street. taken by Messrs. D. Joly & Jas Douglas. 8. Sept. 1819.

House-holder	Occupation	Children	Age above 12	under 12	Total above 12	under 12	Remarks
James Gourlay	Nailor		1				
Bridget Martin	Mother		1				
		Alexr.	1		3		
John Armstrong	Sailor		1				
Wife	- - -		1				
		John		1			
		George		1	2	2	
Alexr. Archibald	Painter		1				
Wife			1		2		
Robt. McKnight	Sailor		1				
Wife			1				
		William		1			
		Mary		1			
		Charles		1	2	3	
Will. Thomson	Joiner		1				
Wife			1				
		James		1			
		William		1			
		David		1	2	3	
John Brydson	Grocer		1				
John McKnight	Apprentice		1				
Grizel do.	Servant		1		3		
Thos. Sproat	Ironmonger		1				
Wife			1		2		
Archibald McClellan	Adjutant		1				
Wife			1				
		Elizabeth	1				
		Mary	1				
		Malcolm	1				
		John	1				
		Margt.	1				
		Ahn	1				
		Jessy		1			
		Thomas		1			
		Dunbar		1			
		Jeanny		1			
Jean Ross	Servant		1		9	4	
Margt. Gordon	Grocer		1				
		Mary	1		2		
Wm. McClymont	draper		1				
Wm. Murray	apprentice		1		2		
John Houston	Flesher		1				
Wife			1				
		Barbara	1				
		Mary	1				
		James	1				
		Margt.		1			
		Marion		1			
Davd. Ewart	Lodger	William	1	1	6	3	
James Saunders	Gaoler		1				
		Robt.		1			
		Nathl.		1			
Margt. Thomson	Servt.		1				
Sarah do.	Servt.		1		3	2	

1819: A NEATLY TABULATED LOCAL CENSUS OF KIRKCUDBRIGHT
(courtesy of Hornel Library & Art Gallery, Kirkcudbright)

2d for Captain David Lauder

N°	Rank.	Names.	From	To		£	s	d	Remarks.
1 2	Captain	David Lauder	25 Aug!	24 Sept!	31	14	11	11	
1 2	Lieutenant	Andrew Hill	do	do	31	8	15	8	
		Alex. Scott	do	do	31	5	15	5	
1 2	Ensign								

Total for Commissioned Officers £ 52 | 3 | 5

N°	Rank and Names.	PAY			Amount Paid									Remarks.
		From	To		£	s	d							
	Serjeants													
1	William Douglas	25 Aug!	24 Sept!	31	2	8	5½						31	
2	Robert Forester	do	do	31	"	"	"						"	
3	William Hay	do	do	31	2	8	5½						31	do
4	John Nicoll	do	do	31	2	8	5½						31	do
5	Alex. Watson	do	do	31	2	8	5½						31	do
6														
7														
	Corporals													
1	George McDougal	25 Aug!	24 Sept!	31	1	16	0¼						31	do
2	William Spittal	do	do	31	1	16	0¼						31	do
3	Robert Watson	do	do	31	1	16	0¼						31	do
4	James Wilson	do	do	31	1	16	0¼						31	do
5														
7														
	Drummers or Fifes													
1	Joseph Low	25 Aug!	24 Sept!	31	1	15	6¼						31	do
2	Alex. Nicoll	do	do	31	1	15	6¼						31	do joined 25 Aug!
3														
4														
5														
	Private Men													
1	Jas. Alexander	25 Aug!	24 Sept!	31	1	11	"						31	do
2	Andrew Beverly	do	22d do	29	1	9	"						29	do
3	Peter Begg	do	24 Sept!	31	1	11	"						31	do
4	William Brown	do	do	31	1	11	"						31	do
5	Robert Brown	do	do	31	1	11	"						31	do
6	Charles Belford	do	do	31	1	11	"						31	do
7	David Belford	do	do	31	1	11	"						31	do
8	John Belford	do	do	31	1	11	"						31	do
9	William Brillie	do	do	31	1	11	"						31	do

1802: A MILITIA LIST FROM ONE OF THE NORTH BRITISH REGIMENTS
(courtesy of Montrose Museum)

William Marr,son,4   E. Lothian, Tranent
Mary Marr, 2   E. Lothian, Tranent

The clues here tell you of an army family. Fort George
is an army base; Chelsea pensioner means military
pensioner, and the children are born where father was
stationed. Even mother's home city is given, helping you
to locate her birth and probably the marriage details.

So don't always moan when you find errors. Errors
sometimes are better than accurate recording.

There is an additional minor difficulty that enumeration
districts did not always remain constant from census to
census. While consistency was preferred, registrars were
invited to suggest alterations at each census, and so
the geographical description at the front of each
enumeration book should be consulted if in doubt.

PRESENT, BUT NOT CORRECT

A person or family that cannot be found may in fact be there, but unrecognised. Some of the data that you now know to be correct may be wrong in the census document, so misleading you. Some people were afraid that if they were paupers they would be sent back to their home parish if they gave the true information in the census.

This was a particular fear in England, where many folk said they were born in the parish they now lived in, to avoid repatriation. If you combine this with a misheard name when the enumerator wrote the facts down for an illiterate head of household, then the combined errors can make it all seem like a different family. It is best to look at the "possibles", and test the members of the family against your known facts. If only one family fits almost all your known facts, then check the same family in the next census, and the anomalies may sort themselves out.

Although we are primarily concerned with the census in Scotland, practically all of it applies equally to England and Wales, the Isle of Man, and the Channel Isles.

English census enumerators were faced with the same situation as their Scottish counterparts, and were just as badly paid - one reason for faint writing in some census records is the cheap ink used. The enumerator had to buy his ink at his own expense for the job, and did not worry about long term considerations. Many of the Scottish returns have this fading ink difficulty, others have been entered with such a fine nib that the thin lines are extremely hard to read on microfilm.

One English enumerator was so incensed that he wrote a diatribe on one of the books complaining about the poor rate of pay for doing a complicated and time-consuming job. In 1851, he was being paid one shilling per 60 persons enumerated, which he reckoned was a 2 to 3 hour task.[letter in Society of Genealogists magazine]

The situation was later improved, and by 1921 the Scottish instructions book for registrars and enumerators lists payment for enumerators as £2.00 plus an extra 8/- per 100 persons enumerated after the first 200, and an additional 1/- per mile travelled above 5 miles in delivering schedules in his district, and the same for collecting the schedules.

THE IRISH ARE DIFFERENT

What our general statements do NOT apply to, however, is the Irish census records. Many of these were destroyed by an arson attack in 1922, and few survived unscathed. The returns for the years 1881 & 1891 were totally destroyed, but 1901 and 1911 were untouched. The returns for 1861 and 1871 have also suffered destruction, but by Government order. These returns were thus destroyed by the "Official" vandals, the others by the "Provisional" vandals! The surviving Irish records are in the Public Record Office of Ireland, Four Courts, DUBLIN 7.

The first attempt at a national census in Ireland was in 1813, but was abandoned before completion. Censuses were then taken from 1821 in the usual ten-year cycle. An interesting aspect of the Irish census is the inclusion of the question of religious affiliation, not asked in Scotland or England. The idea was to find out the proportions of Protestants and Catholics in a very religious country. Protestants were also asked to state their denomination. Only in 1851 was a religious enquiry made in the rest of these islands, and then imperfectly.

For 1851 in Ireland only some parishes in Antrim County plus Drumheeran in Fermanagh County survive; for 1841, only the parishes of Lismore in Waterford County, Killeshandra in Cavan County, and Currin in Fermanagh County; for 1831, parts of Derry County. More of 1821 exists, including parts of Cavan County,, Fermanagh County, Galway County, Meath County, and Offaly County.

Despite this disaster, you can get over it to some extent by virtue of Griffith's Valuation, a survey carried out between 1847 and 1865. It gives the names of all owners and occupiers of land and buildings, and is held by the Irish PRO. It is now available in microfiche form, though the cost may restrict its availability to the largest libraries or universities.

There re also the Tithe Applotment Books (1823 to 1837 period) which list occupiers of agricultural land in each parish, and can be found at the PRO in the North and South as appropriate.

Going further back, there was a Religious Census in 1766, instituted by the Irish House of Lords, when heads of households were listed as Catholic or Protestant. As it was for tithe purposes the poorer section of society is probably missing from this list. The original was destroyed in the 1922 fire in Dublin, but a genealogist, Tenison Groves, had made many transcripts which preserved much of the information.

For a good detailed description of the various census resources to be found in Ireland, see "Irish Genealogy:

a record finder", edited by Donal F. Begley, Dublin, Heraldic Artists Ltd., 1981,repr.1987.

THE USA CENSUSES

The USA is quite good as far as censuses are concerned. The USA has taken federal censuses every ten years since 1790, the intention being to determine population in order to allot seats in the House of Representatives, for those states which were in existence at the time. The early censuses give the head of the household by name, but not the rest of the family. From 1850, each FREE person is listed by name, and the state or country of birth is included. All of the surviving 1790 returns have been published by the US government. The rest were destroyed by fire during the war of 1812. States missing from the 1790 census are Connecticut, Delaware, Georgia, Kentucky, New Jersey, Tennessee and Virginia.

Many of the 1800 and 1810 schedules have been lost, as have some of 1820. If any of your Scots relatives married into an Indian tribe, note that tribes in reservations were not covered by the federal census until 1880. Mid-decennial censuses were taken by a number of States at different occasions, such as in 1885 for the states of Colorado, Florida, Nebraska, and the territories of Dakota and New Mexico. These State censuses often asked different questions, or were more detailed than the federal census, and so can offer a worthwhile extra source.

One point of particular interest is that, whereas in the U.K. the records remain confidential for 100 years, in the U.S.A. this period is only 72 years, resulting in the 1920 records being opened in March 1992. In the case of State censuses, this rule does not apply, so for some states you can see schedules as recent as 1945.

Available for U.S.A. census users is the Map Guide to the US Federal Censuses 1790-1920, by William Thorndale and William Dollarhide (Genealogical Publ. Co., Baltimore, 1987). While quite expensive, its 400 maps help with identifying boundary changes in US counties over the years. These changes in county boundaries were quite frequent, resulting in the same place being in a different county at the next census taking. The maps make the changes quite clear.

There is also for the USA a Census Index Availability Guide, by Andrew J. Morris.(P.O.Box 8825, Fort Collins 80525, 1984).

The U.S. census returns for 1960 are held on some 6,500 computer tapes. This sounds great until you find that they can now only be read by using a make of tape drive that is now out of production. This lesson warns us that census or other data which can be recorded on computer files must only be done using an industry-wide standard

40

format that will be sure to be maintained into the foreseeable future, or until it can be converted into the next industry standard. The advantage of an industry standard is that so many important files in businesses will exist in that format that it will be worthwhile for the computer industry to maintain the usability of these files.

A number of US census records have been published, including, for example, the 1840 census of the Republic of Texas, ed. by Gifford White, (USA, Jenkins, undated) and the 1800 census of Delaware, by Gerald D.O.Maddux (USA, Genealogy Pub. Co., 1964,repr.1976).
More are always being prepared by genealogical societies, so it is worth checking the publication list or newsletters of societies which cover the area where you want to locate a relative.

The chapter on census records in The Source: A guidebook of American Genealogy, edited by A.H.Eakle & J.Cerny (Salt Lake City, 1984) includes details of censuses, whether published or indexed, and location.

For details of state censuses, a full listing is given for each state in State Census Records, by Ann S. Lainhart (Genealogical Pub. Co., USA, 1993).

OTHER COUNTRIES

Of course many other countries have held censuses too, but I do not intend to go into these, except to note the main ones of interest to Scots. There are some books which mention the census records of various countries, and it is worth saying that for Australia there are practically no census records in existence, except for the year 1828 in New South Wales, as government policy is to destroy the returns after extracting the statistics. In Tasmania, census and muster records have survived for 1842 and 1846.

You will be happy to know that the 1828 New South Wales census is published in book form as Census of New South Wales, November 1828, ed. by Malcolm R. Sainty & Keith A. Johnson (Sydney, Library of Australian History,1980, repr. 1985). It is even indexed!

There are still population surveys for Australia, known as Musters because of the military origins, from 1788, but only a few survived in state records, and some only list convicts and not military personnel or free settlers. As usual, it is the criminals who are the best recorded while the good and honest folk get lost in history!

Published examples include General Musters of New South Wales, Norfolk Island, and Van Diemen's Land, ed. by Carol Baxter (Australian Biographical & Genealogical Record, 1987) and General Muster of New South Wales, 1814 (A.B.G.R., 1987). This is part of a continuing publishing programme in Australia, so more will become available.

A similar situation applies in New Zealand, where to all intents and purposes no national census records for individuals exist. I can understand an Australian reluctance to divulge a convict background last century as a reason for wishing destruction of the records by the state, but in New Zealand?? The New Zealand national census has been taken every five years since 1851, keeping detailed statistics only. It is only since 1966 that full returns have been kept, and then only every second census, so that 1966,1976 and 1986 are being kept, but not for public release for 100 years.

However, despite clear instructions for destruction, there are a few surviving census records in the New Zealand National Archives, P.O. Box 805, Wellington: Known survivals are for Nelson, 1845 [SSD 3/1], & 1849 [SSD 3/2], both quite detailed, but naming only the head of the household. The 1849 census of Nelson held by the National Archives (or another version of it) is also held at the Nelson Provincial Museum, and the Alexander

Turnbull Library, National Library of New Zealand, has a photocopy of that.

Related sources include two returns of owners and occupiers of property; one for Auckland in 1845 [IA 1, 45/1939], the other for New Plymouth in 1846 [IA 1 46/153]. All these items are indexed at the National Archives, who will check brief items free of charge.

The National Library of New Zealand tells me that Auckland City Library holds the "Census of the Bay of Islands, May 1846". This is a list of the heads of families only, and covers the Bay of Islands, Hokianga, Kaitaia, Mongonui and Whangarei. That library also holds the "Census Book, Police Office Auckland, 1842 to 1846". It records the name and occupation of each owner, name and occupation of each tenant, along with numbers of family and household by sex, the tenants' occupation by category, and the fabric of the building. It is indexed at the Auckland City Library, and the lists from 1842 to 1845 have been transcribed in Auckland 1842-1845: a demographic and housing study of the city's earliest European settlement, by Martin McLean (N.Z.,1989).

The only national source of note in our context is the Return of Freeholders of land in October 1882, which gives name and occupation of persons. It has been published on microfiche by the New Zealand Society of Genealogists, PO Box 8795, Auckland and is available at some libraries. It may also be held by major libraries in the U.K.

Canada is far better off, with microfilm being available for many of the censuses, and the latest edition of a catalogue of surviving material was published in Ottawa in 1987: Census Returns/Recensements 1666 - 1891, (Ottawa, Canadian Government Publishing Centre, 1987, cat. no.SA2-95/1987). You will also find that a number of indexes to early census exist for places like Nova Scotia, primarily being heads of household indexes.

The earliest census records in Canada are those for the French settlements, from the late 17th century, and the records get fewer and more recent the further west you go, following the gradual pattern of European population movement across the country. The far west territories only start with the 1881 returns.

The British Columbia Genealogy Society has got over this by publishing Heads of Households in B.C. in 1874, ed. by Pet Vibert (British Columbia Genealogy Society, 1984), a compilation of names from directories and electoral lists. There are also published indexes, by Lorne Main, to the 1881 censuses of British Columbia (B.C.G.S., 1982); Manitoba & East Rupert's Land (B.C.G.S.,1984); Northwest territories and Algoma, Ontario (B.C.G.S.,1984), and also a surname index by Eric Jonasson to the 1870 census of Manitoba and Red River (B.C.G.S., 1984).

We are also lucky with Ontario, as not only do the census records go far back, but there are also many indexes available. You can save a lot of time by going direct to the census indexes and searching them for your relative, and the information you want is well laid out in the excellent little book Indexes to Ontario Census Records: an inventory, by Norman Kenneth Crowder (Ontario Genealogical Society, 1987).

South Africa had census surveys in 1897, 1904, 1912,and 1921, which might be of use, but a genealogist friend of mine found that South Africa was a dreadful country to deal with as far as genealogical records are concerned. Noel Currer-Briggs, in his book Worldwide Family History (Routledge & Kegan Paul, 1982) says little about censuses in South Africa, except to mention that in Natal there are only statistics, no original returns. The only avenue worth exploring if you are interested in South Africa is that a genealogical society was established in 1964, and it publishes information on genealogical sources in their quarterly journal, Familia.

Gibraltar, though British, is unhelpful for census material. The first count was done in 1878, then 1881 onwards at ten year intervals. The records are not available for public inspection, and mostly do not show individuals' names.

Another British possession, Surinam, was the subject of a census in 1811 while under British rule, and this, which distinguishes the various racial populations, survives in the PRO file Surinam Original Correspondence, etc. [CO 278].

Some European countries appear to be quite good for census records, other countries less so.

Norway held a census in 1769, then 1801, then 1815, and every 10 years until 1875. It restarts in 1890 on a ten year basis. 1875 and 1900 are in regional archives, the rest in national archives. Names are used from the 1801 census, and from 1865 the place of birth is included.

Denmark starts in 1787 and up to 1911 is in the P.R.O., Copenhagen. Police census lists from 1866 to 1923 are in the Copenhagen City Archives. Finland started censuses in 1635, and these are held in the national archives. Iceland also has census records going back two centuries in their archives, their first census being taken in 1703. Sweden took its first census in 1749.

In France, the first census was in 1590, but very few family details were noted. National censuses start in 1801, as in Britain. They are good from 1832, but some have been destroyed in wartime this century. Censuses were takem at approximately 5 year intervals, but most returns give numbers and not names within a household, until 1926 when name, forename, age and occupation are given. There were variations between administrative Departements in earlier records. Census records for each Departement are held at the Archives Departmentales. The Paris departement census records (from 1832) are held at the Archives de Paris, 18 Boulevard Serurier, 75019 Paris. Related material includes Liste Recrutement (recruitment lists) from about 1879, listing men aged from 20 and eligible for military service: quite detailed about individuals. Registres Matricules (military censuses) do not start till after 1902, but include date and place of birth.

Belgium started census recording in 1846, and every ten years since. Their census records are held on microfilm and can be consulted in Brussels and Louvain la Neuve.

Germany has had irregular local censuses, and as these are held in various State archives and not centralised they are not readily accessible.

Switzerland held a city census in Berne in 1764, then a federal census in the various states from the 1836/38 period. From 1860 there are complete census records, and they are held in the State Archives, Berne.

Malta, being a British possession for a considerable period, held its first census in 1842, then 1851, and every ten years as in the UK, with the same gap in 1941. Their records are held by the Public Library, Valetta. Many other countries have begun censuses, but most only in the last 100 years. Some countries such as Ethiopia and Lebanon have still no census.

NOT EXACTLY A CENSUS - BUT A LIST IS CLOSE

What we should not ignore is census material other than the official government ones, or at least something equivalent to a census. By this we mean a list of local people comprehensive enough to include either most of the population, or at least the heads of each household. One type is Listings of Inhabitants, and consist primarily of local surveys done for specialist purposes and which have survived to provide us with useful material, particularly when they pre-date the state census.

The primary reason for a list of inhabitants in most parishes was for religious purposes. In Scotland this was used by the minister to check that he was visiting all the families in his parish, in order to ensure that those above a selected age knew the catechism by rote. They are variously known as visitation lists, examination rolls or catechismal rolls.

These are almost as good as a census because the children were all listed, because if they were not old enough at the time to examine, their names were noted for the future. An example of this is my Craig parish by Montrose, 1788 and 1791 (Aberdeen & N.E.Scotland Family History Society, 1986,repr. 1990). The 1788 part is a transcription of a listing of inhabitants of the type described, held in the S.R.O.[CH2/616/14], with people divided into Under 8 and Over 8. Clearly 8 was the minister's selected age for examination eligibility. Many more of these lists are now becoming available.

North East Scotland Library Service has microfilm of most of the surviving lists relating to its area. This includes Birse parish, where there is a succession of lists from 1789 to 1825, [SRO-CH2/595/11,12], and Dunnottar parish for 1834,[SRO-CH2/110/11].

A list of the inhabitants of Glentanar in 1812 gives all the names under each farm or estate, a total of 311 persons, of whom 232 were of catechisable age (10 years old) and 79 under 10. The list also notes that in 1762 there were 282 of catechisable age, and in 1760 there were 260. The whereabouts of the original list is unknown, but a later typed copy now in private hands allowed the Aberdeen & N.E.Scotland F.H.S. to publish the full list in their journal No.40 (Sept. 1991).

Aberdeen University's Department of Manuscripts & Archives holds a list of inhabitants of Old Meldrum, 1741. It is among the estate papers of the Duff family, and lists 351 heads of households. An alphabetical list of the names appeared in Journal 19 (summer 1986) of Aberdeen & N.E.Scotland Family History Society.

The Shetland Archives have a number of lists of inhabitants of various dates, (listed in their directory entry). Strathkelvin Libraries hold a List of Householders for the parish of Cadder dated 1797.

The manuscript of an Arbroath roll dated 1752, arranged by street or locality, is held by the Signal Tower Museum in Arbroath, and has now been published as Examination Roll of Arbroath 1752, Town's Duty Roll 1753, edited by Flora Davidson, M.A. (Scottish Record Society, 1988).

A very useful list for Cambuslang, 1807, is to be found in James A. Wilson's A History of Cambuslang, published in 1929.

Examples of other rolls known, mostly in S.R.O., are: West Kirk, Edinburgh, 1632-1639, [CH2/718/210]; Canongate, 1661,1684,1687,1699, [CH2/122/67,68,98]; Duddingston and part of Canongate, 1699,1700-1703,[CH2/125/2]; St. Cuthberts, 1729-30 & 1790, [CH2/718/212] & [CH2/718/211]; South Leith, 1740-1763, [CH2/716/327, 328], all Edinburgh; Uphall, West Lothian, 1660-1670, [CH2/362/1]; Liberton, Midlothian, 1683,1692,1694, [CH2/383/3]; Inveresk, Midlothian, 1687-90, 1741, 1744, 1749, 1755, [CH2/531/54,55]; Kinross, 1710-11 (in private hands); Lochrutton, Kirkcudbright, 1728-1746, 1759-1763, 1766-1789, and some in the 19th century, [SRO transcripts: RH2/8/55-68]; Gretna, Dumfries, 1730, (in parish); Rothesay, Bute, 1771, 1818, 1820, & 1816 [SRO:GD1/456/92,192,200, & 235], 1775,1776,1814(photocopy),1815(Bute Museum); Lesmahagow, Lanark, 1783,[Nat. Lib. of Scotland, Ms.8230]; Kippen, Stirling, 1789-1791, 1793-94 (held in the parish); Moulin, Perth, 1804, [CH2/488/19]; and Kilfinan, Argyll, 1837, [OPR 518/1].
Those which give the fullest listing of inhabitants are: Lochrutton in 1766, Kippen, Birse, and St. Cuthberts.

Another parish examination register in private hands - that of New Abbey, Kirkcudbright, 1744-1763, held by the Minister of New Abbey, will I hope be in print before too long.

In Kirk Session minute books you may very well find long lists of names in the form of a communion roll. Do not regard that as in any way a complete list of the adults. Unlike today, you had to be "worthy" to take communion in earlier times, and these communion rolls were fairly exclusive in most cases, tending to debar the poor and other unworthy folk.

All lists have to be looked at in the correct context, like the Extent Rolls for Edinburgh, 1635, in Edinburgh City Archives. These were drawn up for an annuity tax to pay ministers, and so must be viewed in that light. I doubt if the local paupers were included in the list, unless only to exempt them!

One of the earliest of these censuses is for the Burgh of Stirling, listing 385 men and women, apparently householders, recorded at the back of a volume of Stirling Burgh Court and Town Council Records,1544-50, held by Central Region Archives[B66/15/2]. The list is undated, but recorded after an entry dated 5 July 1552, so was presumably compiled after this date. Unfortunately there is no explanation for the list, though it may have been drawn up for taxation purposes. You can refer to the content of this list in an article in the Scottish Antiquary, vol.VI, pages 175 to 178. Another whose purpose is uncertain is: List of the whole inhabitants of Perth, March 1766, now in Perth & Kinross District Archives [B59/24/1/36].

Now an even earlier list has come to light. Newly translated documents forming part of the Walter Mason Collection of Historical Documents have revealed a list of householders living in Stow, Midlothian, in 1530. The documents, in the hands of Ettrick & Lauderdale Museum Service, cover the entire Borders area. The museum holds other archives of great interest, such as a valuation list of the Burgh of Selkirk,1714, a cess book for the same burgh, 1794-1845, and militia lists for the County of Selkirk, 1815-1831. A trust fund has been set up to support, conserve, and exploit the material.

The 1682 Constables' List of the householders of Edinburgh, North and South Leith and the Canongate was drawn up for a levy on households to finance a guard for the town. 1684 is the dating of Parish Lists of Wigtownshire and Minnigaff, edited with indexes by William Scot, (Scottish Record Society, Edinburgh, 1916).

The Rev. David Landsborough,(1779-1854), well known as a naturalist, also kept a visiting work-book for his parish of Stevenston, Ayrshire, and this includes a list of inhabitants at the end of 1819 and start of 1820. The list is by street, with names of those living in each house, with occupations, but no ages or relationships. His 1822/24 list merely lists the husbands and wives at each address, but the 1835/6 list includes occupations, population figures, and numbers of children under 7, and under 12. The work-book, part of the extensive Alexander Wood Memorial Collection, is held by the Local History department of Cunninghame District Libraries HQ.

Another interesting private census was the 1779 list of the inhabitants of the Duke of Argyll's Estates, (Scottish Record Society, 1963) with a further list in 1792. Their coverage includes Kintyre, Morven, Mull, Tiree and Iona, and also Roseneath in Dunbartonshire. The originals remain at Inverary Castle.

Blair Castle has its own archive, including censuses of the Duke of Atholl's estates, 19th century to 1909, and also a list of fencible men, 1705/6.

Over 2,000 names appear in lists of able-bodied men in 1745 in the Sutherland parishes of Kildonan, Creich, Farr, Rogart, Loth, Clyne, Dornoch, Golspie & Lairg. The lists are geographically arranged, and held by the National Library of Scotland among the Sutherland estate papers [Dep.313/3248]. The volume of Sutherland Estate Management Papers published by the Scottish History Society includes a census of the inhabitants of Culmaily (Golspie), 1810, which names the 52 heads of the family, with numbers in the family.

Another item recently uncovered is a list of the population of Rothiemurchus parish in 1837. It was among the Grant of Rothiemurchus estate papers and was noted by the National Register of Archives (Scotland) as part of its ongoing work of noting locally-held archives.

One survey entitled The Inhabitants of Kincardine Moss [SRO:GD1/321/1] is, however, nothing to do with Kincardineshire, but rather an estate in Perthshire which was settled in a reclamation experiment. The list is dated 1814 and the settlers were mainly highlanders, but a good deal of detail is included in the list, even mentioning those who had died, giving cause of death and age at death.

Early lists of this kind exist elsewhere too. There is a surviving local census for the parish of Ealing, in England, in 1599, in the P.R.O., London [series E.163-Exchequer miscellanea], and I have noted mention also of censuses for the baronies of Newcastle and Upper Cross, County Dublin, circa 1652.

Should you find no local census material for the area or period you seek, then use the less complete lists such as early valuation rolls or voters' lists. Many of these exist, and are a whole area of interest in themselves. You should find local ones in the same repositories as most of the census materials. A few are mentioned for interest within the directory at the end of this book.

MILITARY MUSTER ROLLS

These sources can be a list of the serving men of a
military force, or can be lists of men eligible to be
called up for service in the local militia. Some are
sparse in names, covering only the officers, others are
complete listings of all personnel.

A few are mentioned here to give a flavour.

The Roll of the Earl of Argyll's Regiment for January
1690, [SRO,E100/14] gives the names of the privates
together with the parishes and counties from which they
came, and their occupations. Most came from Argyllshire,
but some from as far as Aberdeenshire. The majority came
from around Inverary.

Montrose Museum holds an 1802 and 1803 payroll list of
the Forfar and Kincardineshire Militia which lists all
soldiers, officers and men alike.

Another, much earlier military manuscript of interest
is: Pay of the Forces from Fines and Cess 1665-1702
[SRO,E91/1] which includes a list of officers.

The Ewart Library, Dumfries, has muster rolls for the
Dumfries Militia, 1799-1815, and other lists; and
Aberdeen City Archives has a Militia Ballot List for Old
Machar, 1828. There are probably more in other archives.

The Scottish Record Office has many early Scots muster
rolls, most of which are fairly uninformative
genealogically, but one muster roll which is
exceptionally good is the Roll of the Troop of
Lifeguards of June 1678 [E100/6/1], which lists all
ranks, parentage, place of birth, and length of service.

Rolls for these early periods are not usually so good,
and the S.R.O. does not hold those for Scottish
regiments in the British Army. These are held by the
Public Record Office, Ruskin Avenue, Kew, Richmond,
Surrey, TW3 4DU. A useful introduction to the PRO is
Tracing your ancestors in the Public Record Office, by
Jane Cox and Timothy Padfield, (HMSO, 1981).

Some muster rolls may be found in published form,
usually within military histories, such as John
M.Bulloch's Territorial Soldiering in the North-East of
Scotland during 1759-1814 (Aberdeen, New Spalding Club,
1914). This work includes lists of officers, and
sometimes enlisted men, found in various muster rolls.
In the case of the Gordon Highlanders in 1794, the roll
states the name of the soldier, his age, height,
birthplace, trade, and career details, if any. The men
come from all over the country, although Aberdeenshire
and Banffshire predominate.

Muster rolls and pay lists are according to the

regiment, and from about 1868, at the end of some musters, there is a marriage roll listing wives and children for whom married quarters were provided.

An unknown number of militia lists exist among private papers throughout Scotland, but some of them can be tracked down through the surveys done by the National Register of Archives (Scotland). These surveys record brief details about archives held in local hands, but as many of the bundles of papers get the description "Miscellaneous papers", there are probably more lists still to be identified. Some are more clearly listed, such as those of the Earl of Annandale and Hartfell, [Survey no.2171] which include a bundle noting muster rolls of the Earl's company and troop, 1667 & 1689; a number of other undated troop lists and muster rolls, and miscellaneous accounts and discharges relating to Annandale's troop, 1650-89.

These lists are often the only opportunity for finding male ancestors without property in the 17th century.

Military records constitute a field in themselves, where you might be able to trace a man from enlistment, where his age may be stated, to his discharge or death, when his birthplace, trade, and date of enlistment should be mentioned at the end of the quarter's muster.

Rolls of the regiments of Bonnie Prince Charlie's army in the 1745 rebellion can be found in the Muster Roll of Prince Charles Edward Stuart's Army, 1745-46, edited by Alastair Livingstone, Christian Aikman, and Betty Hart; (Aberdeen University Press, 1984). In it, for example, can be found under the Forfarshire (Ogilvy's) regiment, names, ages, occupations, and home town or village, and whether transported, deserted, etc. "David Gouck (20), servant, Montrose. Transported".

A detailed examination of the Seaforth Muniments by Sir Mervyn Medlycott recently revealed that they include Posse Comitatus Lists dated 1798 for most of Ross & Cromarty, listing all able-bodied men aged 15-60 not already in military occupation. It totals 6,600 names, covering all parishes EXCEPT Cromarty, Kilmuir Easter, Kintail, Tain, Urray and Isle of Lewis. [SRO, GD46/6/45]. There are also Militia Ballot Lists of all men aged 19 to 23 in 1797 for the whole county of Ross, including the Isle of Lewis, but excepting the parishes of Fodderty, Knockbain, Lochalsh, and the old county of Cromarty [SRO:GD46/6/38].

The Seaforth Papers also include a list of heads of households in Ness parish, with the number of persons in each family.

Regimental museums have some relevant papers, but a recent survey unearthed surprisingly few. Fort George looks to be the best such source for Inverness and Ross Militia.

For more detailed information on Scottish muster rolls,
I can recommend Militia Lists and Muster Rolls, 1757-
1876, by Jeremy Gibson & Mervyn Medlycott (FFHS, new
edition due late 1993), and for the earlier period
Tudor and Stuart Muster Rolls, by Jeremy Gibson & Alan
Bell (FFHS,1989).

TAX ROLLS

To conclude this listing of lists, or census of
censuses,it may be worth mentioning in brief some
government records held in the SRO. There you can find
tax lists drawn up by government officials to make sure
people paid their taxes, just as now. Not everyone was
covered by these taxes, because of exemptions and other
reasons, so they cannot be looked on as other than a
poor substitute for census records. They as usual are
mainly lists of householders, or at least the head of a
family. Such records are so profuse, but difficult to
use effectively for family history, that the best
solution is to call at the SRO and detail your area of
interest. A specific place and time can narrow down the
search and elicit some reasonable help from an already
busy staff at the SRO. You must come properly prepared,
knowing exactly who, and what, you want to find, or you
may waste your time and that of others.

The major series of tax lists is the Assessed Taxes
Schedules, which begin in 1717, when by the Act 20 Geo
II cap.3, duplicates of all the assessments were ordered
to be transmitted to the office of the King's
Remembrancer to ensure they conformed to the Act. The
extant schedules cover Window Tax, 1748-1798,
Commutation Tax (additional duties on houses and
windows), 1748-1798, Inhabited House Tax, 1778-1798,
Shop Tax, 1785-1789; Servants Tax (duties on male
servants), 1777-1798, Female Servants Tax, 1785-1792;
Cart Tax (on carts and wagons), 1785-1792, Wheel
Carriage Tax (those with two wheels and four wheels),
1785-1798; Horse Tax (on carriage and saddle horses),
1785-1798, Farm Horse Tax, (workhorses and mules), 1797-
1798; Dog Tax, 1797-1798, Clock and Watch Tax, 1797-
1798; Aid and Contribution Tax, 1798-1799; Income Tax,
1799-1802.

Following the Consolidating Acts, the duties on windows,
inhabited houses, male servants, carts, carriages, and
dogs were incorporated in comprehensive Assessed Taxes
Schedules, Income Tax and later Property Tax remaining
on separate schedules. No Property Tax schedules have
been preserved, and comprehensive Assessed Tax schedules

only exist for 1798-99, but there are Assessed Taxes and Property Tax Schedules for Midlothian, 1799-1812 [E.920]. Midlothian is also well served by another series of similar records [E.327].

From 1748-1759 assessments are by district, thereafter by county, with separate schedules for royal burghs, the schedules apparently being kept in yearly bundles.

It is probably best to consider approaching most of these national tax records as a last resort, due to the minimal amount of information likely to be found on individuals.

Inevitably, there is an exception to this general statement on government tax records. It is the Hearth Tax. The Scottish Record Society have published:West Lothian Hearth Tax 1691, With County Abstracts for Scotland (with separate index), ed. by Duncan Adamson; (Scottish Record Society, 1981). As well as giving the tax lists for the county , there are statistical notes and commentary about the other Scottish counties, parish by parish, so this can be a guide to the suitability of hearth tax records in your research. As a census substitute, it leaves much to be desired, but it does at least give most of the heads of households even in many cases where they would be exempt from the tax.

The same details of the Scottish hearth tax lists are found in The Hearth Tax, Other Later Stuart Tax Lists and the Association Oath Rolls, compiled by J.S.W.Gibson, (F.F.H.S., 1985, reprinted 1990).

For Aberdeenshire and Kincardineshire, microfilm of the 1693/4 hearth tax records is held in the local history dept., NESLS, Oldmeldrum. The originals are not easy to read, as I found when I looked at them in the S.R.O., and the microfilm does not make it any easier, so do not anticipate too much from such early records unless you have some knowledge of the writing styles of the period.

Copies of the Bute hearth tax rolls, 1693 and 1694, are held by Bute Museum, Rothesay.

St. Andrews University Library holds poll tax returns for St. Andrews and Anstruther, 1697/8, as well as Stent Rolls for some East Fife Burghs up to 1857.

Local tax lists can be more productive, and the Dumfries Archive Centre has an excellent collection of local material of this nature, including Police Tax lists (1795-1887, with gaps) of heads of households, sometimes in alphabetical order, sometimes by street, and sometimes just as lists of those who have paid or in arrears. They also hold Stent rolls (1718-1839 with gaps) and other lists of taxpayers in the period 1805-1865.

One published tax list, known as the Poll Book of Aberdeenshire - List of Pollable Persons within the Shire of Aberdeen, 1696 (The Spalding Club, Aberdeen, 1844) is available in public libraries and is being gradually reprinted in manageable sections, indexed for the first time, by the Aberdeen F.H. Society, putting another useful resource into our hands. Some poll tax material is known to exist for other areas, but incomplete and unpublished. Aberdeenshire is the only complete example.

AN EARLY ABERDEEN CENSUS

The Poll Book and its use in family history came to public notice last century, and stimulated the journal "Scottish Notes and Queries" to publish in June and July 1893 a local census of Old Aberdeen which was taken in 1636, one of the earliest on record. The Aberdeen F.H. Society hopes to publish this census, laid out in a more usable form.

It was compiled by an order of the "Court of the Citie of Auld Aberdeine", which was dated the 11th of May. The order declares "The said day was taken up ane roll of the haill inhabitantes of the Auld toun Chanrie and Spittel thair bairnes and servandes. As also ane roll of all the poor folkes within the said Toune and parioche". The population as listed totals 235 adult males and 324 adult females, and after adding the unnamed "bairnes" the final population at this census was 836.

An example of an entry is "Alexander Moubray, his wyff, his dochter, and his tua oyes." The next two entries are "Janet Woode, vidow", and "Cristiane Con, hir dochter, and Elspet Philp, hir servant".

From this we see that the head of the household is the named person, followed by numbers of the rest of the family, then names of servants. While limited in identifying people, it does help in providing a family group, and is especially good in listing all the servants by name.

Many of the heads of household have their occupation listed, which is a useful extra, but you may have to find out what that occupation actually is - there are many wobsters, plus the occasional muxter,baxter, puddinwricht,laxfisher, and commer! My own favourite entry is "Peter Barnet, his wyff and thrie uther strang women". I'm not sure if "strang" here is strong or strange!

The best strategy is to check such sources for your family name, and take notes for future reference. When you have exhausted the official census records, you have to rely on every possible avenue to supplement the Old Parish Registers, and build up a picture of your family, or possible members of your family.

And that is what this research is all about: getting access to sources, and using them to best advantage. I hope that this description of census resources encourages you to investigate this avenue further than you have tried so far, and make useful discoveries for your own family history.

LIBRARY AND ARCHIVE SOURCES
FOR CENSUS MATERIAL IN SCOTLAND

Bodies whose replies have indicated no relevant material have been omitted from the directory unless their inclusion helps to avoid wasted enquiries by others.

Please note that the information given is as supplied at the time of enquiry, shown as (1/93) for January 1993. More material, e.g. microfilm, may now be held than shown in the entry.

Aberdeen City, Arts and Recreation Division, Library Services. Local Studies Dept., Central Library, Rosemount Viaduct, Aberdeen AB9 1GU. Tel.0224-634622, ext.225, Fax.0224-641985.
Holdings of census microfilm 1841-1891 for Aberdeen City, Aberdeen County, Kincardine County; also, Banff County parishes: Marnoch, 1861; Mortlach, Ordiquhill, 1861-1871; Rathven, tRothiemay, 1841-1871, 1891; St. Fergus, 1841-1891; Seafield, 1861-1891.
Census indexes - Street index for Aberdeen city, 1851, 1861, 1871, 1881, 1891.
Postal enquiries - willing to transcribe an entry. where a name and parish, (in Aberdeen City a street address) is provided.
Microfilms are readily available. Readers are not bookable, but a time limit of one hour is applied at busy times. Since other items may need to be fetched from store, advance warning of a visit is advisable.
Photocopies: A4-10p, A3-20p; printouts from microfilm of newspapers only - 10p per A4 sheet.
Open Mon.- Fri. 9am-9pm; Sat. 9am-5pm. (2/93)

Aberdeen City Archives, Town House, Aberdeen AB9 1AQ, Tel.0224-522513/ 0224-276276 ext.2513, Fax.0224-644346.
Holdings include a list of subscribers to the Board of Relief 1639/40, and an almost complete set of listings by precinct of male inhabitants aged over 16 compiled for militia purposes in 1759.
Main holdings are stent rolls for Brurgh of Aberdeen for 42 years between 1576 and 1670, for 1707 plus a few in early 19th There are also Police rate rolls for 1795,1797, and 1800-1860. There is a valuation of 1712.
Communtation road assessment books are held for 22 years between 1806 and 1841, Aberdeen Road District.
Other material includes Police assessment rolls for a few years between 1832 and 1850, and voters registers between 1832 and 1855.
Postal enquiries to above address. Staff can offer advice but do not undertake detailed searches.
Photocopies 12p per A4 sheet.
Booking is advisable for personal visits, particularly if travelling from a distance.
Open: Mon. 10.30am-12.30pm, 2pm-4.30pm; Tue. to Fri. 9.30am-12.30pm, 2pm-4.30pm. (11/93)

Aberdeen University. Queen Mother Library, Meston Walk, Old Aberdeen, Aberdeen AB9 2UE, Tel.0224-272579, Fax.0224-487048.
No census microfilm held, nor other relevant material, except early voters lists, Aberdeen 1832 and 1838. "We do not do research; if enquiries very specific we will simply confirm details".
No charges except photocopies - 10p + VAT per A4 sheet.
Open:(term) Mon.- Thu. & Sat. 9am-10pm, Fri.9am-5pm, Sun.2pm-10pm; (vacation)Mon.-Fri.9am-5pm, Sat.9am-1pm. (2/93)

Aberdeen University. Department of Special Collections and Archives, Kings College, Aberdeen AB9 2UB, Tel.(enquiries) 0224-272598, Fax. 0224-487048.
Holdings: 1741 list of householders, Oldmeldrum [mss 2778/10/18](transcript in Aberdeen F.H.S. Journal No.19, Summer 1986). Visitors by appointment. Archival photocopier available.
Open: Mon.-Fri.9.30am-12.30pm,1.30pm-4.30pm (2/93)

Angus District Libraries & Museums. Libraries with census material: Arbroath, Brechin, Carnoustie, Forfar, Kirriemuir, Montrose.
Holdings of census microfilm 1841-1891 for all Angus (Forfarshire) parishes except Dundee City area. Contact local libraries direct. Enquiries by post should be specific. Archives enquiries via Montrose Library.
No research charges, but enclose an s.a.e. Library & museum hours are being standardised.
Montrose Library, High St., Montrose, Tel.0674-73256 holds microfilm and an archival transcript of the Forfarshire Hearth Tax roll,1690, plus indexed stent rolls for Montrose for 1797,1809,1829; Hospital pension rolls, 1735-1794. Archivist also has an indexed 1822 Forfarshire militia oath book.
Forfar Library, West High St., Forfar Tel.0307-66071 holds an Index of Forfar shoemakers 1626-1813; Index of Forfar weavers, 1627-1836.; 1690 Forfar Hearth Tax (indexed), and 1689 inventory of the cornes destroyed by General Mackay (indexed).
Brechin Library, St. Ninian's Sq., Brechin, Tel.03562-622687 holds the Roll of Burgesses, 1710-1974.
Arbroath Library, Hill Terrace, Arbroath DD11 1AH, Tel.0241-72248, holds typescript index of persons from the Protocol Book of John Colville, Arbroath 1775-83; Typescript register of qualified voters for the Burgh of Aberbrothwick 1832-57; Printed lists of Burgesses/ electors for town council, Arbroath, 1831,41,44,49, 50-55; Alphabetical lists of burgesses 1789-1902; Parish of Arbroath 1901 & 1906, accounts for parish council with a list of poor relieved and other statistics; Arbroath and St. Vigeans parish council observations on the poorhouse books, 1912.
Arbroath Museum, Signal Tower, Ladyloan, Arbroath DD11 1PU, tel.0241-75598, has Mss. Arbroath parish examination register of 1752 (now published).
Open: Mon.-Sat., 10am-5pm.
Montrose Museum, Panmure Place, Montrose DD10 8HE,

Tel.0674-73232: Payroll of Forfar & Kincardine Militia, 1802/3 (lists all soldiers in various companies of the 8th Regt. North British Militia, Mar/Apr.1802, and of the 11th Regt.,Aug/Sep.1803. index in prep.); a few voters rolls, earliest is 1716, and other archives. Likely delays to written queries, but all answered if A4 width s.a.e. enclosed. Personal callers helped if reasonable notice given. The originals of some local archival items remain with the archivist.
Open: Mon-Sat., 10am-5pm. (3/93)

Arbroath: William Coull Anderson Library of Genealogy, Dewar House, Hill Terrace, Arbroath DD11 1AJ. Tel.0241-76221, ext.240. Operating within the Angus District Libraries, a Trust Fund finances this special library, which offers a commercial genealogy service.
Holdings include census microfilm - Aberlemno, Airlie, Arbirlot (1851,61); Arbroath, Montrose, Murroes, Newtyle, Oathlaw, Panbride, Rescobie, Ruthven, St. Vigeans, Stracathro, Strachan, Tannadice, Tealing (1851-71); Garvock, Glenbervie, Kinneff & Catterline, Laurencekirk, Maryculter, Marykirk, Nigg, St. Cyrus (1861); Aberdalgie (1861,71); Auchterhouse, Barry, Brechin (1861,71); Carmyllie (1861); Aberfeldy, Aberfoyle, Abernethy, Abernyte, Alyth (1871).
Typescript indexed copy of 1851 census Carmyllie.
Open: Mon.-Fri.,9-12;1.30-5. (1/93)

Argyll & Bute District Libraries, Library HQ., Hunter St., Dunoon PA23 8JR, Tel.0369-3214 & 3735.
No census holdings, but happy to receive postal enquiries for other family history material.(2/93)

Ayr. Sub-office of Strathclyde Regional Archives, Regional Offices, Wellington Square, Ayr KA7 1DR.
Holdings include church documents for Presbytery of Ayr, transmitted from SRO, including lists: Kirkoswald, 1831 list of parishioners [CH2/562/27]; St. Quivox, parish population report, 1821 [CH2/319/22]; communicants rolls and/or heads of families for parishes of Dailly, Ballantrae, Coylton, Monkton, Ochiltree, various dates; and Dundonald parish statute labour lists, circa 1824.
Estate papers of Kennedy of Kirkmichael include a list of heads of household for Kirkoswald parish,c.1690 [ATD42/7/6] and several lists of people appearing before the Bailliery Court of Carrick in 1677 [ATD42/7/2-4] and 1717 [ATD42/7/10].
Open: Wednesdays only, 10am-1pm, 2pm-4pm. (1/93)

Bearsden & Milngavie District Libraries. Brookwood Library, 166 Drymen Road, Bearsden G61 3RJ. Tel.041-942-6811. Fax.041-943-0200.
Holdings of census microfilm: 1841 - parishes of Dumbarton, Kilmaronock, Kirkintilloch, Luss, New/E. Kilpatrick;
1851 - Luss, New/E. Kilpatrick, Old/W. Kilpatrick, Roseneath, Row;
1861 - Kilmaronock, Kirkintilloch, Luss, New/E. Kilpatrick, Old/W. Kilpatrick, Roseneath, Row;

1871 - Luss, New/E. Kilpatrick;
1881 & 1891 - New/E. Kilpatrick.
Postal enquiries answered free of charge, unless
extensive photocopying required. Microfilm photocopies
at 10p/sheet.
Open: Mon.- Fri. 10am-8pm, Sat. 10am-5pm. (1/93)

Blair Castle Archives, Blair Atholl, Pitlochry,
Perthshire PH18 5TL, Tel.0796-481207, Fax.0796-481487.
Holdings: Main censuses of the inhabitants of Duke of
Atholl's estates are 1867, 1882, and 1909. There are
various 19th century lists of parts of the estate, and
also a List of Fencible Men, 1705/6.
The archive can be visited by prior appointment but only
on weekdays. There is a charge for both visiting and
obtaining written answers to enquiries, which varies
depending on the nature and amount of information
sought. (1/93)

Borders Regional Library Service: Archive & Local
History Centre, Regional Library H.Q., St. Mary's Mill,
Selkirk TD7 5EW, Tel.0750-20842, Fax.0750-22875.
Holdings of census microfilm 1841 - 1891 complete for
counties of Berwickshire, Roxburghshire, Peeblesshire,
and Selkirkshire, plus parishes of Stow, Fala and
Soutra, Temple, Heriot, Glencorse and West Calder.
Leaflet on Archive & Local History Centre. Mainly local
authority archives. Postal & personal callers.
Appointment advised for microfilm use.
No charges except photocopies.
Open: Mon.-Thur. 9am-1pm, 2pm-5pm; Friday 9am-1pm, 2pm-
4pm. (1/93)

Bridge of Weir History Society has a transcription from
microfilm of the 1851 census return for Houston parish,
which covers Bridge of Weir. Transcript is held by Mrs.
M. Howison, 7 Horsewood Road, Bridge of Weir PA11 3BD,
Tel.0505-690803. (2/93)

Bute Museum, Stuart Street, Rothesay PA20 0BR (1/4 mile
from pier) has a library with many local archives,
including Rothesay examination rolls for 1775 &
1776(owned by the High Kirk), 1814 & 1815; copies of
Bute hearth tax rolls, 1693,1694; Inhabitants of Bute
liable for statute labour on roads, 1791; List of
householders served notice re local militia, 1809.
This is a small, privately run museum. They have no
telephone, but postal queries are accepted. Visitors for
research, by appointment with Hon. Librarian/archivist.
No photocopier.
Entry charges: Adults-70p, O.A.P-40p, children-20p.,
further donations welcome.
Open: Oct.-Mar.,2.30pm-4.30pm; Apr.-Sep.,10.30am-
12.30pm,2.30pm-4.30pm.(3/93)

Central Region Archives, Unit 6, Burghmuir Industrial
Estate, Stirling FK7 7PY, Tel.0786-50745.
Holdings: census microfilm: Stirlingshire- Airth & Alva
1851; Baldernock, Balfron, Bothkennar, Falkirk, Larbert,

Muiravonside, Polmont, Slamannan, & Strathblane 1841 & 1851; Buchanan, Campsie, Denny, Drymen, Dunipace, Fintry, Gargunnock, Killearn, Kilsyth, Kippen, St. Ninians 1841; Stirling 1851. Perthshire- Blairgowrie, Callander & Caputh 1841 & 1851; Cargill, Cluie, Comrie & Crieff 1841; Blackford,Blair Atholl& Strowan 1851. Printed Census Reports for Stirlingshire, 1911,21, 51,61,71; Clackmannanshire, 1931, 1951. Examination rolls of Buchanan [Inchcailloch], 1714-21, 1722-1728, 1733-46, and 1759; Alva Kirk Session visiting book, 1854-1857; local militia rolls, various dates 1854-1888. List of Stirling Burgh householders, circa 1552, in vol. of council records[B66/15/2]. Advise advance booking of microfilm reader. Free initial research for written genealogical enquiries. Photocopies: 30p. Open: Mon. - Fri., 9am-5pm. (1/93)

Clackmannan District Libraries: Alloa Library, 26/28 Drysdale Street, Alloa FK10 1JL. Holdings of census microfilm: Parishes of - Airth, Alloa, Alva, Clackmannan, Dollar, Muckart, Tulliallan, Tillicoultry, Trinity Gask, Weem, 1841-1891; Logie (inc.Menstrie), 1841-81; and a number of other parishes on the same film reels. No published list. Postal & personal callers. Photocopies 5p, printouts 10p. Only basic searches by staff. (1/93)

Clydesdale District Council. Lindsay Institute, Hope St., Lanark, ML11 7LZ, Tel.0555-661339, Fax.0555-665884. Holdings of census microfilm 1841-1891, for local parishes as follows: Biggar, Carluke, Carmichael, Carnwath, Carstairs, Covington, Crawford, Crawfordjohn, Culter, Dolphinton, Douglas, Dunsyre, Lamington, Lanark, Leadhills, Lesmahagow, Libberton, Pettinain, Quothquan, Roberton, Symington, Thankerton, Walston, Wandel, Wiston. The reels also contain other parishes outside the library's area. Roll of Freeholders of the County of Lanark, 1831, with a list of electors for County of Lanark for 1839 - this has handwritten amendments for 1840-1842. It gives name, occupation, status, property & address. Lists of persons entitled to vote in Burgh of Lanark for 1850-1855 and 1879. Also, statistical local data in "Upperward Almanacks" from 1871 onwards. 2 microfilm readers and 1 fiche reader available without charge at present, but book in advance of arrival. Postal enquiries dealt with, particularly for overseas enquirers, but not genealogical research as such. No published list. Personal callers preferred. Please enclose s.a.e. A contribution towards photocopying costs is appreciated (payable to Clydesdale District Libraries). Open Mon.- Wed. & Fri. 9.30am - 7.30pm, Thu. & Sat. 9.30am - 5pm. (1/93)

Cumbernauld & Kilsyth District Council. Local Collection, Central Library, 8 Allander Walk, Cumbernauld G67 1EE, Tel.725664, Fax.0236-458350.
Holdings of census microfilm, 1851: Arrochar, Bonhill, Cardross, Cumbernauld, Fintry, Gargunnock, Killearn, Kilsyth, Kippen. 1861: Dunbartonshire: Arrochar, Bonhill, Cardross, Cumbernauld, Dumbarton; Stirlingshire: Falkirk, Fintry, Gargunnock, Killearn, Kilsyth, Kippen. 1871: Arrochar, Bonhill, Cardross, Cumbernauld, Killearn, Kilsyth, Kippen, Larbert, Muiravonside, Polmont. 1881: Dunbartonshire: Cardross, Cumbernauld; Stirlingshire: Kilsyth, Kippen.
Postal enquiries to confirm an entry only, where location given. (1/93)

Cumnock & Doon Valley District Council. Library H.Q., Council Offices, Lugar KA18 3JQ. Tel.0290-22111:
Holdings: census microfilm 1841-1891 for local parishes and others in Ayrshire (list available).
Only one microfilm reader, so you should book for a half-day session in advance.
Open Mon.-Fri. 9am-4.30pm. (1/93)

Cunninghame District Libraries: Local History Dept., 39-41 Princes Street, Adrossan KA22 8BT, Tel. 0294-69137, Fax. 0294-604236.
Holdings of census microfilm: Fairly complete for Ayrshire parishes in District, 1841-1891, including Arran and the Cumbraes.
Available for consultation as part of the large Alexander Wood Memorial Collection are David Landsborough's Visiting Workbooks for Stevenston (including lists of inhabitants in 1819/20, 1822/24, 1835/6).
There are lists of genealogical sources held. Brochure due 1993.
Postal enquiries acknowledged immediately, thereafter dealt with as soon as possible (early 1993 backlog is 4-5 months).
Photocopies/printouts 10p per page.
Personal callers by appointment, Mon.- Fri.,9.30am-5pm. (1/93)

Dumbarton District Libraries. Dumbarton Public Library, Strathleven Place, Dumbarton G82 1BB, Tel.0389-63129.
Holdings of census microfilm 1841-1891 for whole of Dunbartonshire East and West, i.e. parishes of Arrochar, Bonhill, Cardross, Cumbernauld, Dumbarton, Kilmaronock, Kirkintilloch, Luss, New Kilpatrick, Old Kilpatrick, Rhu[Row] and Rosneath. Some Stirlingshire and Argyllshire parishes included in these films.
Census indexes: 1851 Arrochar, Luss, Rosneath - alphabetical lists giving full census data for each name. 1861 Street/Building indexes for Bonhill, Cardross, Dumbarton, and Row[Rhu]. 1871 Head of Household/Male employed index for Cardross. 1891 street/building/named houses indexes for Bonhill, Dumbarton, and Row.
Other indexes - All McGregors in Dunbartonshire

parishes, 1851 census; Indications of legibility of microform of enumeration books for Dunbartonshire, 1861 and 1871; Listings per street of name of household, occupation, no. in household, no. of rooms, for 1861 census of Dumbarton for Dennystown and part of High Street, and similarly for 1871 census of Dumbarton, for Dennystown, and for 1881 census of Dumbarton for Newtown.
Some voters rolls of Dumbarton, from as early as 1841, and directories for Dumbarton and adjacent parishes for 1877,1885 and 1892. Directories for Helensburgh - incomplete run from 1836 to 1950s. Recent valuation rolls and voters rolls for the whole District and complete runs of valuation rolls for Cardross and Helensburgh from beginning of 1900s.
Postal enquiries accepted. No charge if easily answered from indexes, etc., but local studies librarians will charge £5 per hour where the enquiry involves searching unindexed material.
Publication: "Lennox Links"- guide to genealogical resources in Dumbarton District, includes detailed census holdings list. (1/93)

Dumfries & Galloway Regional Libraries. 1851 census, on microfiche, available at libraries in Stranraer, Newton Stewart, Castle Douglas, Dalbeattie, Lockerbie, Annan, Georgetown, and the Ewart Library, Catherine St., Dumfries DG1 1JB. Tel.0387-53820/52070, Fax.0387-60294. Also held are Militia enrolment lists for Dumfries Militia, 1804 [D9/3/1] and for Wigtownshire, 1821-31 [W7/1/1]; and Muster Rolls for Dumfries Militia, 1799-1815 [Strongroom XIV, box 3]. (1/93)

Dumfries Archive Centre. See Nithsdale District Council.

Dundee District Council. Archive & Record Centre, 21 City Square, Dundee DD1 3BY, Tel.0382-23141 ext.4494. Visitors, by appointment, come to 1 Shore Terrace, at rear of City Square.
Holdings: Population of the Town, 1801 [Town Clerk's Misc., no.57] (indexed); Longforgan, Perthshire - scroll returns, 1811(indexed), 1821, 1831, 1841 [P/Lo 4].
Callers can consult archives free of charge. Outline list available. Postal enquiries to City Square.
Open: Mon.-Fri., 9.15am-1pm;2pm-4.45pm (1/93)

Dundee District Council. Central Library, The Wellgate, Dundee DD1 1DB, Tel.0382-23141, ext.4338, (26115 after 5pm and Sat.), Fax.0382-201117.
Holdings of census microfilm: Dundee 1841-1891. Other parishes as follows: Careston,1851; Cortachy & Clova, 1851; Coupar Angus, 1851; Craig, 1851; Dun, 1851-71; Glenprosen, 1851; Kinettles, 1841; Kirkden, 1841,1881; Kirriemuir, 1841,51,81; Lethnot, Navar, Liff Benvie & Invergowrie, Lintrathen, Logie-Pert, Lunan, Lundie & Fowlis, Mains & Strathmartine, Maryton, Menmuir, Monifieth, Monikie, all 1841-81; Montrose, 1841-71; Murroes, 1841-71; Newtyle, Oathlaw, Panbride, Rescobie, all 1841,51,81; Ruthven, 1851,81; St. Vigeans,

Stracathro, Tannadice, Tealing, all 1881.
Printed street index for Dundee for 1841-1891. Recently compiled is a name index for the 1841 Dundee census. Postal enquiries for specific searches (given year, street, and no. if a long street).
No charge for enquiries. Personal callers can obtain printouts from reader-printer at 75p per sheet; photocopies - 16p (under review).
Local History Dept. open: Mon., Tue., Fri.,Sat. 9.30am-5pm; Wed. & Thu. 9.30am-7pm. (1/93)

Dundee University Library and Archives, Dundee DD1 4HN, Tel.0382-23181, Fax.0382-29190.
Holdings: No census microfilm. Certain volumes of the statistical returns, 1871 onwards.
S.J.Jones "The 1841 Census of Dundee; its value as source material for the historical geography of Dundee", Univ. of Dundee, Dept. of Geography Occasional paper No.3, 1975[Per 910.5].
Michael Anderson - The 1851 census: a national sample of the enumerators' returns, Chadwyck-Healey,1987 [Microfiche 312.094 2A548].
Growing local collection includes family history material. Postal and other enquiries accepted. (1/93)

Dunfermline District Libraries. Holdings at Central Library, Abbot Street, Dunfermline KY12 7NW, Tel.0383-723661, Fax.0383-620761.
Holdings of census microfilm, 1841 - 1891, for at least 50 parishes in Fife, Perth & Kinross.
Publication: "Tracing your ancestors - a guide to sources in the Central Library" (1981). (3/93)

East Kilbride Libraries. Central Library, The Olympia, East Kilbride G74 1PG, Tel. East Kilbride 20046.
Holdings of census microfilm: Lanarkshire parishes - 1841-1891: Avondale, Blantyre, Cambuslang, Carmichael, Carmunnock, Douglas(only part in 1861), Dunsyre, East Kilbride, Glassford. 1841-71:Bothwell, Cadder, Carnwath, Carstairs, Covington & Thankerton, Crawford, Crawfordjohn, Culter. 1841-71,91: Biggar, Govan(part). 1841-61: Barony(part), Cambusnethan. Also, Carluke 1841-61,81,91; Dalserf 1841,51,71(part); Dalziel 1841,51, 71,81(part); Dolphinton 1841,51,71-91; Glasgow (part) 1861-71; Hamilton 1841-51; Stonehouse 1851. Renfrewshire parishes - 1841-91: Cathcart, Eaglesham, Mearns. Also, Eastwood 1841-71,91; Erskine 1851-71,91; Lochwinnoch 1841-51,91; Neilston 1841-71.
Surname index for 1881 East Kilbride. Place-name index 1841-1891 for East Kilbride in preparation.
List of Cambuslang, 1807, available in "A History of Cambuslang" by James A. Wilson (Glasgow,1929).
Two film readers (no printouts), films on open access, no booking system. Photocopier. Postal enquiries accepted. No charges.
Open: Mon.,Tue.,Thur.,Fri.,9.45am-7.45pm; Wed.,Sat.: 9.45am-5pm. (2/93)

East Lothian District Libraries. Local History Centre, Haddington Library, Newton Port, Haddington EH41 3NA, Tel.062-082-2531.
Holdings of census microfilm: 1841-1891 for all parishes in East Lothian. Other material: Valuation rolls from 1899 on microfiche; East Lothian yearbooks from 1820; local newspapers on microfilm.
Postal enquiries accepted only for quick searches for specific information. No charge made. Personal callers can reserve 3 hours at microfiche/film reader in advance.
Useful leaflet on the Local History Centre's material. Photocopies A4 -10p.
Centre open: Mon. 2pm-6pm; Tues. 10am-1pm, 2pm-7pm; Thur. & Fri. 2pm-5 pm. (2/93)

Edinburgh City Archives, Dept. of Administration, Edinburgh District Council, City Chambers, High Street, Edinburgh EH1 1YJ, Tel.031-529-4616, Fax.031-220-1494. No census records held, but holds original local tax returns dating from 18th & 19th centuries. Closely specified postal enquiries accepted, plus personal callers (by appointment on first visit).
Photocopies: 28p plus VAT per copy.
Open: Mon.-Thu. 9am-4.30pm, closed Fridays. (1/93)

Edinburgh District Council. City Libraries: Scottish Department and Edinburgh Room, Central Library, George IV Bridge, Edinburgh EH1 1EG, Tel. 031-225-5584.
Holdings of census microfilm 1841-1891: Edinburgh Room holds Edinburgh City; Scottish Department holds East, West & Midlothian, Peeblesshire, Roxburghshire, Berwickshire, Dumfries, Galloway, Fife, Kinross, Clackmannan and Ayrshire.
Street indexes available for Edinburgh only.
Postal enquiries accepted but limited to specific queries. No charge made.
Personal callers welcome but may have to wait to use microfilm viewers - no booking system available.
Both departments open: Mon.-Fri. 9am-9pm; Sat.9am-1pm. (1/93)

Edinburgh: Registrar General for Scotland, New Register House, Edinburgh EH1 3YT, Tel.031-314-4441,031-314-4427, Fax.031-314-4400.
Holdings: all census returns for Scotland that exist, 1841 to date, but only 1841 to 1891 may be consulted.
Free general advisory leaflet (SU/1) and list of fees.
Searches by staff: minimum data required is the name of the person and the full address of residence at the census date.
Personal searches: normally by using microfilm copies. Seats may be reserved, and it is particularly advisable to make a booking if travelling any distance to Edinburgh. Search places booked in advance must be occupied before 10.00am (unless a reason is given when booking), and further details of booking arrangements can be obtained be telephone (direct line 031-314-4433). If not booked in advance, arrive at 9 am or earlier to

have a good chance of a seat.
Charges: For personal searches, all records (including census) - £15 per day or part day; search by staff for specified entry in a census - £5. Copies of census extracts (£11.00 in person, £14.00 by post) are additional. Postal enquiries: pay by cheque, postal order, Visa or Mastercard, not cash. Any refunds are by sterling cheque, amounts under £2.50 will not be refunded because of cost.
Purchase: copies of census records 1841-1891 on 35 mm. microfilm are available for purchase through the Microfilm Unit, room 15 (direct line 031-314-4425). Films are only sold as complete reels of up to 100 ft, and often contain more than one enumeration district on the reel. Ask for quotation, but current charge (from 1.4.93) is £35 per reel (including VAT), plus a handling charge of £3 per order. Supply can take some time for larger orders. (1/93)

Edinburgh University Library, Special Collections Dept.
Holdings:Islands of Rum, Eigg, Muck & Canna, 1765, in David Laing Collection.

Ettrick & Lauderdale Museum Service, Municipal Buildings, High Street, Selkirk TD7 4JX, Tel.0750-20096, Fax.0750-23282.
Holdings: archives including the Walter Mason Collection with a number of interesting lists including: Householders in Stow, Midlothian, 1530; Militia Lists for the County of Selkirk, 1815-1831; Burgh of Selkirk Cess Book, 1794-1845; Valuation list of the Burgh of Selkirk, 1714. Consultation by appointment.
No entry fee. Charges only for postages and photocopies.
Open: Mon.-Fri., 9am-5pm. (2/93)

Falkirk District Libraries. Falkirk Public Library, Hope Street, Falkirk FK1 5AU, Tel.0324-24911, ext.2316.
Holdings of census microfilm: Airth, Baldernock, Balfron, Bo'ness, Bothkennar, Buchanan, Campsie, Carriden, Dalmeny, Denny, Drymen, Dunipace, Ecclesmachen, Falkirk, Kirkliston, Muiravonside, 1841-1891; Abercorn, Bathgate, Livingston, St. Ninians,1841-1871; Kippen, 1841-71,91; Gargunnock and Queensferry,1841,61,71; Killearn,1841,61,71,91; Fintry and Slamannan,1841,61-91; Larbert, 1841,61,81,91; Stirling 1841,1851,1871; Polmont 1841,81,91; Linlithgow 1841,1891; Strathblane, Torphichen, Uphall, 1841; Dollar, Whitburn 1851; Grangemouth 1881,1891; Haggs 1891.
No published list. Postal enquiries for specific queries only. Photocopies: A4:15p/sheet.
Open: Mon.,Tue.,Thur. 9.30am-8pm; Wed.,Fri.,Sat. 9.30am-5pm. (3/93)

Glasgow District Libraries. Mitchell Library, North Street, Glasgow G3 7DN, Tel.041-221-7030, Fax.041-204-4824.
Holdings of census microfilm: Glasgow 1841-1891,

complete with street indexes for each census year.
Staff will assist readers with personal enquiries and answer phone and letter enquiries, but only to a limited extent.
Self-service copies. Fiche printer: A4-25p/sheet, Film printer: A3-50p/sheet, A4-25p/sheet. Copies from microfilms can be ordered, made on electrostatic machine (A3 size -£1.60, but can also do A4 to A1). Sterling prepayment normally required.
Library open: Mon.-Fri. 9.30am-9pm, Sat.9.30am-5pm. Closed Sundays. (1/93)

Glasgow City Archives:See Strathclyde Regional Archives.

Glasgow University Archives. No census microfilm or other census material held.

Grampian Regional Archives. Old Aberdeen House, Dunbar St., Aberdeen AB2 1UE. Tel.0224- 481775.
Local authority archives for all former authorities in area, but no census material held. Photocopies A4 and A3 - 15p. each.
Open: Mon.-Fri. 10am-1pm, 2pm-4pm. (2/93)

Hamilton District Libraries. Hamilton Central Library, 98 Cadzow Street, Hamilton ML3 6HQ, Tel.0698-282323, ext.143.
Holdings of census microfilm for various parishes in Lanarkshire, 1841-91.
Place/street index (1841-1881) for parishes within Hamilton District (Blantyre, Bothwell, Dalserf, Hamilton and Stonehouse) indicating census district numbers for named houses, streets, farms and villages.
Personal enquirers welcome but no booking system for microfilm readers. Postal enquiries for specific queries only.
Leaflets on family history material, and census/OPR holdings.
No charges at present, except for photocopies. Microfilm prints, (subject to copyright restrictions): A4-20p. Photocopies: A4-10p.,A3-20p.
Open: Mon.,Tues.,Thur., 9.30am-7.30pm, Wed.,9.30am-1pm, Sat.,9.30am-5pm. (1/93)

Heriot-Watt University. The University Archive, Heriot-Watt University, Riccarton, Edinburgh EH14 4AS, Tel.031-449-5111, ext.4064/4140, Fax.031-451-3164.
Holdings: printed census reports for G.B.,1851; Scotland, 1861.
Gibson-Craig of Riccarton papers (15th to 19th centuries) containing estate papers, musters, rentals, testaments, etc., mostly relating to the Currie/Balerno area, 17th to 19th centuries.
Postal enquiries.
Personal visits by appointment (Tel.031-449-5111, ext. 4064).
No charges except copying/incidental expenses. (5/93)

Highland Regional Council - Highland Regional Archive.
Inverness Library, Farraline Park, Inverness IV1 1NH,
Tel.0463-220330, Fax.0463-237001.
Holdings of census microfilm: 1841-1891 for Counties of
Caithness, Sutherland, Ross & Cromarty, Inverness,
Nairn, Argyll, (property of Highland F.H.S.).
Holds census indexes belonging to the Society.
Sutherland County census statistics 1801-1831.
1811 census records for parishes of Assynt, Farr and
Golspie (householders named).
Genealogist in residence provides brief introduction to
sources and guidance in use of records freely, detailed
consultations and answering of enquiries are charged at
the rate of £11.50 for the first hour, £20.70 for 2
hours, and £34.50 for 3 hours. The charges are inclusive
of V.A.T. but do not include payments for photocopies
(15p/sheet; 50p for copies from reader/printer).
Highland Regional Archive open: Mon.-Fri.,9am-5pm,
visitors are by appointment. (3/93)

Inverclyde District Libraries. Watt Library, 9 Union
St., Greenock PA16 8JH. Tel.0475-20186, Fax.0475-882010.
Holdings: 1841-91 census microfilm for Renfrewshire.
Street index for 1841-1891 for Greenock, Port Glasgow,
Gourock, Kilmacolm and Inverkip; a name index for Port
Glasgow, 1841-91. A name index for Greenock is in
preparation.
Photocopying 20p/sheet. General access, and postal
queries welcomed.
Open: Mon. & Thur. 2pm-5pm, 6pm-8pm; Tue. & Fri. 10am-
1pm, 2pm-5pm; Wed. & Sat. 10am-1pm. (1/93)

Kilmarnock & Loudon District Libraries. The Dick
Institute, Elmbank Avenue, Kilmarnock KA1 3BU, Tel.0563-
26401,Ext.128, Fax.0563-29661.
Holdings of census microfilm: 1841-1891 for all parishes
in Ayrshire.
Other material of note: Kilmarnock Midwife's Register,
1777-1829(approx.); Kilmarnock Mortality Register,1728-
1763 (approx.); Kilmarnock directories from 1833; Local
newspapers from 1844.
Leaflet - "Tracing Your Family Tree - sources in the
Dick Institute".
Postal searches of census material only if definite
information to work on, and delays likely.
No photocopies from census, no charges.
Personal callers Mon.Tue.Thu.Fri. 9am-8pm, Wed.& Sat.
9am-5pm. (2/93)

Kirkcaldy District Libraries. Local History Department,
Central Library, War Memorial Grounds, Kirkcaldy, Fife
KY1 1YG, Tel.0592-260707.
Holdings of census microfilm: 1841-871 for
Abbotshall (1881,91 are in Kirkcaldy parish); 1841-1891
for Aberdour, Anstruther, Arngask, Auchterderran,
Auchtertool, Ballingry, Beath, Burntisland, Cameron,
Carnbee, Carnock, Crail, Dalgety, Dunfermline, Dunino,
Dysart, Elie, Falkland, Ferryport-on-Craig, Flisk,
Forgan, Inverkeithing, Kemback, Kennoway, Kettle,

Kilconquhar, Kilmany, Kilrenny, Kingsbarns, Largo, Leuchars, Logie, Markinch, Monimail, Moonzie, Newburgh, Newburn, Pittenweem, St. Andrews & St. Leonards, St. Monans & Abercrombie, Saline, Scoonie, Strathmiglo, Torryburn, Wemyss; 1851-1891 for Abdie, Auchtermuchty, Balmerino, Ceres, Collessie, Creich, Cults, Cupar, Dairsie, Dunbog, Kinghorn, Kinglassie, Kirkcaldy, Leslie.
List available of census & OPR held.
Postal & Tel. enquiries. Charges only for printouts or photocopies. (1/93)

Kirkcudbright: E.A.Hornel Art Gallery and Library, Broughton House, Kirkcudbright DG6 4JX, Tel.0557-30437.
Admission: Adults-£1.50, O.A.P.-£1, Children -50p.
Home of the artist E.A. Hornel (1864-1933) who collected rare books and manuscripts, mainly local.
The 20,000-volume Library includes a Kirkcudbright Burgh Census, 1819 (all named), and a census of the Parish of Balmaclellan, Kirkcudbrightshire, 1792 (all named, with ages).
Other items of interest are: Roll of Assessment for Relief of the Poor of Kirkcudbright parish, 1848 to 1856; List of arrears due by tenants in the Barony of Sanquhar and Barony of Drumlanrig, 1744; Stewartry of Kirkcudbright Licence Book, 1772-1831; 1st Kirkcudbright Rifles Squad Book, 1862, and other interesting lists.
Research fees - £8 per day; brief enquiries - photocopy charges only.
Postal enquiries preferred, but brief enquiries by unannounced visitors are possible.
Open from Easter until mid-October as follows: Mon.-Sat.(except Tue.), 11am-1pm,2pm-5pm, Sun. 2pm-5pm.(3/93)

Kyle & Carrick District Libraries. Carnegie Library, 12 Main St., Ayr KA8 8ED, Tel.0292-269141,ext.5227, (after 4.45pm - 286385), Fax.0292-611593.
Holdings of 1841-1891 census microfilm for the district council's area and a number of other Ayrshire parishes (detailed holdings list available). Two microfilm reader/printers available, which can be booked for 2-hour periods, up to 2 weeks in advance. Printout service available.
Many other name lists held, including feu registers for Troon, 1834-1894; list of voters for the County of Ayr, 1857, for South Ayrshire, 1877 & 1883; some Ayrshire directories from 1829; The Patriotic Fund, 1854 (lists of donors in each Ayrshire parish).
Postal and personal enquiries welcome.
Open: Mon.,Tue.,Thu.,Fri., 9am-7.30pm, Wed. & Sat., 9am.-5pm. (2/93)

Midlothian District Libraries. Local Studies Collection, now moved (1993) to: 2 Clerk St., Loanhead EH20 9DR, Tel.031-440-2210.
Holdings: census microfilm 1841-1891 for the whole of the former County of Midlothian.
Photocopies of Lasswade Parish Church: 1) Roll of Communicants and adherents, Nov.1875, and 2) Allocations

of Sittings, Nov.1886.
Transcription of 1694 Poll Tax is almost complete for
parishes NOW in Midlothian plus Heriot, Stow and
Inveresk. Newton parish has no 1694 record.
Publication: useful leaflet "Local Studies Collection".
Library also reprints local books and maps.
Postal and personal callers. Viewer/copier available.
No charges except for photocopies: A4-10p, A3-20p.
Open: Mon. 9am-5pm,6pm-8pm; Tue.-Thur. 9am-5pm; Fri. 9am
-3.45pm. (1/93)

Monklands District Libraries. Local History Department,
Airdrie Library, Wellwynd, Airdrie ML6 0AG, Tel.0236-
763221, Fax.0236-423950.
Holdings: census microfilm 1841-1891 for Airdrie,
Coatbridge, and vicinity.
Microfilm copies of Airdrie valuation rolls from 1855 to
1943, and for Coatbridge, 1885-1943.
Postal and tel. enquiries welcome.
No charges, except for photocopies [A4-10p, A3-20p] and
postages.
Publications: Free leaflets "Family History-Trace your
Ancestors" and "Local history-a guide", which
incorporates a list of local publications for sale,
including "Population of the Monklands", by P.Drummond.
Open: Mon.Tues.Thur.Fri., 9.30am-7.30pm; Sat. 9.30am-
5.00pm; closed Wed. (6/93)

Moray District Archives: within Moray District
Libraries. Holds 1811 census of Dallas, all named, with
ages.

Moray District Libraries. Elgin Library, Grant Lodge,
Cooper Park, Elgin IV30 1HS, Tel.0343-2746.
Holdings: census microfilm 1841-1891 for Banffshire,
Moray, and Nairn, plus certain parishes in Aberdeenshire
and Inverness-shire of various dates.
Photocopies of manuscript censuses - Mortlach,
1805,1821; Dufftown, 1820,1826; Glenrinnes, 1901.
Personal name indexes to: St. Andrews-Lhanbryde,1841;
Birnie,1841-1881; Aberlour, Banff, Boyndie, Fordyce,
Gamrie, Marnoch, Mortlach, Ordiquhill, Rathven,
Rothiemay, all 1851.
Printed census reports, Great Britain, 1811,1861,1871.
"Status animarum" of the Catholic families in parish of
Bellie, 1808.
Free leaflet-"Tracing your roots in Moray" details
resources. Personal callers welcomed. Postal enquiries -
limited searches.
Open Mon.-Fri. 9.30am-8pm, Sat.10am-noon. Photocopies
10p & 20p. (1/93)

Motherwell District Council. Museums & Heritage
Service, Motherwell Library, Hamilton Rd., Motherwell
ML1 3BZ, Tel.0698-251311.
Holdings: Census microfilm 1841-91 for Shotts,
Cambusnethan, Bothwell and Dalziel parishes; 1841-1881
for Hamilton . A place name index is available for
these. Other microfilms held: Biggar, Blantyre, Carluke,

Dalserf, Stonehouse, Symington, Walston, Wandell/
Lamington, Wiston/Roberton, 1841-1871; Cadder,
Cambuslang, Pettinain, Rutherglen,1841-1861; Carmichael,
Carmunnock, Carnwath, Carstairs, Crawford, Crawfordjohn,
Culter, 1841-51; Covington, 1841; Douglas, Dunsyre,
Dolphinton, East Kilbride, 1841,61,71; Thankerton, 1851.
Postal enquiries accepted.
No charges except for photocopies.
Open: Mon.,Tue.,Thu.,Fri. 9am-7pm, Wed. 9am-noon,
Sat.9am-5pm. (1/93)

National Library of Scotland. Department of Manuscripts,
George IV Bridge, Edinburgh EH1 1EW, Tel. 031-226-531
& 031-459-4531, Fax. 031-220-6662.
Holdings: Mss. drafts of 1881 & 1891 census of Kames
Castle, Bute [MS.15923,ff81,93].
Inhabitants lists: Invergarry, 1861-70, 1871-72
[MS.15164-5 & 15166] - all named in Glengarry &
Glenquoich estates.
Examination rolls: Lesmahagow, 1783[MS.8230]; Colinton,
1780 [Adv. MS.20.3.11]; Musselburgh, n.d., (18th
century) [MS.17868].
List of property owners and occupiers in Golspie
Village, 1850 [in Acc.10225]; Lists of able-bodied men
in Sutherland parishes 1745 [Dep.313/3248], plus militia
lists and muster rolls among the Sutherland Papers,
Minto Papers, etc.
Printed reports on the census from 1801 to 1911, held
among their British Parliamentary Papers.
The library does not have staff to handle detailed
postal enquiries, or offer much assistance to personal
callers, but there are catalogues available to consult.
General leaflet on the Dept. No charges. (2/93)

Nithsdale District Council. Dumfries Archive Centre, 33
Burns St., Dumfries DG1 2PS, Tel.0387-69254.
Holdings of census microfilm: 1841-1891 for all
Dumfriesshire, Kirkcudbrightshire and Wigtownshire
parishes. A good proportion of 1851 returns is being
produced as a persons index, parish by parish, jointly
with local f.h. society. Copy of published Annan census
1801-21. Printed census abstracts 1841 & 1851; 1951 for
Dumfriesshire & Kirkcudbrightshire.
The Centre's "Source List 7", and supplement, give
details of material of genealogical interest, including
many name lists from militia rolls and tenant lists to
police tax assessments.
Genealogical research cannot be undertaken by the
archivist, and other postal enquiries must be specific.
Personal callers welcome, but a booking must be made in
advance stipulating whether a microfilm/ microfiche
reader is required. No charges.
Opening hours: Tues.,Wed., & Friday, 11am-1pm,2pm-5pm;
Thursday evening 6pm-9 p.m. (1/93)

North East Fife District Libraries. Cupar Library, 33-35
Crossgate, Cupar KY15 5AS, Tel.034-53722.
Holdings of census microfilm 1841-1891: Anstruther
Easter & Wester, Cameron, Carnbee, Crail, Dunino, Elie,

Falkland, Ferryport-on-Craig (Tayport), Flisk, Forgan (Newport-on-Tay), Kemback, Kettle, Kilconquhar, Kilmany, Kilrenny, Kingsbarns, Largo, Leuchars, Logie, Monimail, Moonzie, Newburgh, Newburn, Pittenweem, St.Andrews & St. Leonards, St. Monance (Abercrombie), Strathmiglo. The following parishes are lacking 1841, otherwise complete to 1891: Abdie, Auchtermuchty (also lacks 1881), Balmerino, Ceres, Collessie, Creich, Cults, Cupar, Dairsie, Dunbog.
Other useful holdings: The Register of voters for Fife 1832; Fife shop keepers and traders, 1820-1870, compiled by A.J.Campbell; Fife deaths from the files of Fife newspapers, 1822-1854, compiled by A.J.Campbell.
Postal enquiries - research charge £7.50 per hour. Personal callers - book in advance for use of microfilm reader. Family history leaflet. Photocopying from microfilm or bound newspapers - 50p per copy.
Cupar library open: Mon.,Tues.,Wed.,Fri., 10am-7pm; Thurs.,Sat., 10am-5pm. (2/93)

North East of Scotland Library Service. Local History Dept., Admin. H.Q., Meldrum Meg Way, The Meadows Industrial Estate, Oldmeldrum, Aberdeenshire AB5 0GN, Tel.0651-872707, Fax.0651-872142.
Holdings of census microfilm: 1841-1891 for all Aberdeenshire, Kincardineshire, and parts of Banffshire now in Banff & Buchan District. Local duplicates at Fraserburgh, Strichen, Peterhead, Ellon, Huntly, Inverurie, Kemnay, Macduff, Stonehaven, and Inverbervie. H.Q., Fraserburgh, Peterhead, Stonehaven and Strichen can do printouts.
Also held: 1811 & 1821 census microfilm for Dunnottar parish. Minister's examination rolls (list of inhabitants) for Birse, 1789 up to 1825 (approximate ages given in 1791); Dunnottar 1833,1835,1837, all on microfilm at H.Q. (Originals in S.R.O.)
Leaflet on family history material; list of holdings of census microfilm at service points; list of newspaper holdings.
Charges: photocopies and printouts 10p. personal searches free. Postal queries: First half hour of staff time free, then £8 per hour or part hour.
H.Q.(Local History Dept.) open: Mon.- Fri., 10am-5pm. Other libraries at branch opening times. Booking essential at H.Q. & Stonehaven, advisable elsewhere. (4/93)

Orkney Islands Council. Archives Dept., The Orkney Library, Laing Street, Kirkwall KW15 1NW, Tel.0856-873166, ext.24 or 25.
Holdings: 1841-1891 census microfilm for all of Orkney; 1821 census returns for St. Andrews, Deerness, South Ronaldsay, Burray, Swona, Pentland Skerries, Stromness and Sandwick parishes (all named, with ages); 1821 List of Inhabitants for Orphir parish (all named, with ages).
Photocopying: 15p(A4); 25p(A3); 60p(A2).
Postal enquiries for specific items only. Personal visits by appointment. Normal hours: Mon.-Fri. 9am-1pm, 2pm-4.45pm. (1/93)

Perth & Kinross District Libraries. Sandeman Library, 16 Kinnoull Street, Perth PH1 5ET, Tel. 0738-23329, Fax. 0738-36364.
Holdings: census microfilm for Perthshire and Kinross-shire, 1841-1891. Advance booking preferred.
Printed census statistics for 1801,1831,1851-1991, except 1921 and 1941.
Charges for use of microfilm: £1.00 per hour for those living outwith Perth & Kinross District.
Library accepts postal queries, but makes a research charge of £10.00 per hour for all enquiries originating outside the library authority's area.
Photocopying charges:A4-10p, A3-30p. Reader/printer copies from microform:A4-50p,A3-£1.00.
Library open: Mon.-Wed. 9.30am-5pm; Thu. & Fri. 9.30am-8pm; Sat. 9.30am-1pm.
District Archive (Address, Tel. & Fax. as for library).
Holdings: List of heads of households in Perth City for 1766, and an incomplete list of inhabitants for 1773, both indexed by surname.
Archive open Mon.-Fri. 9.30am-5pm. (2/93)

Renfrew District Council. Paisley Museum (NOT Library), High Street, Paisley PA1 2BA, Tel.041-889-3151.
Holdings of census microfilm: complete County of Renfrewshire, 1841-1891. Because on same film, some parishes in Ayrshire, Bute, and Argyllshire also held.
Staff have compiled a street index to the censuses for Paisley and Paisley Abbey parishes. Greenock parishes also indexed by a volunteer.
Specific postal and/or telephone enquiries dealt with as quickly as possible.
No research charges at present.
Open: Mon-Fri., 10am-4.45pm, and by special arrangement on Sat. at same times. Pre-booking is essential (sessions 10-1.30;1.30-4.45; or full day). (6/93)

Roxburgh District Museums, Hawick Museum, Wilton Lodge Park, Hawick, Roxburghshire TD9 7JL, Tel. 0450-73457.
Holdings include "Registered Voters of the County of Roxburgh, October 1835" [divided into parishes and listing names, profession & residence]; Valuation Book of the County of Roxburgh, printed 1811.[owners of land and value in Scots pounds]; and "Analysis of the Valuation Books of the County of Roxburgh, June 1788", with quotes from valuation books of 1643 and 1678.
Written enquiries to Curator, at above address.
Charges: Finding fee of £2 to £5 if the enquiry takes more than half an hour. Photocopies at 5p/sheet.
Museum open: April-Sep., Mon.-Sat. 10am-12noon,1pm-5pm, Sun. 2pm-5pm; Oct-Mar.,Mon.-Fri. 1pm-4pm, Sat. closed, Sun. 2pm-4pm.

St. Andrews University Library, North Street, St. Andrews, Fife KY16 9TR.
Holdings: Census microfilm (in Manuscript dept.) - All Fife parishes 1841-1881, except those (mainly 1841) which do not survive.
Abdie, Fife, 1821 census & Burgh of St. Andrews, 1838

(householders named in both).
Printed volumes of census reports for 1831(in Rare Books dept.), 1861, 1871, 1881, 1891 (all Scotland), and reprints of 1801,1841, 1851 (Great Britain).
Stent Rolls for some East Fife Burghs, up to 1857 (in Manuscript dept.). Poll tax returns, 1697/98 for St. Andrews and Anstruther.
Postal enquiries accepted if straightforward. Personal visits for more complicated inquiries. No charges.
Open: Mon.-Fri. 9am-1pm,2pm-5pm; Sat. (termtime only) 9am-12.15pm. (1/93)

Scottish Catholic Archives, Edinburgh. No census material. Does NOT hold any genealogical material, as Roman Catholic registers are kept by the local dioceses. Does not wish genealogical enquiries. (1/93)

Scottish Record Office, H.M. General Register House, Princes Street, Edinburgh EH1 3YY, Tel.031-556-6585, Fax.031-557-9569. Historical Search Room for consulting archives at this (main) site, and West Search Room at West Register House, Charlotte Square, Edinburgh (modern records, and maps and plans are among the materials here).
Please note that census records 1841 onwards are all held by the Registrar General at New Register House, next door (See full entry under Edinburgh).
Holdings: The S.R.O. is valuable for pre-1841 surviving original parish returns, and census equivalents e.g. lists of inhabitants, Ministers' examination rolls, some very early military muster rolls, later militia ballot lists and posse comitatus lists, hearth tax, poll tax, and other tax records.
Free leaflets available: "Facilities for historical research" and "Family History", detailing the types of records available and how they may be consulted.
Apply in person (identification needed) for a reader's ticket, valid 3 years . As many records are no longer stored centrally, and may have to be brought into the city centre search rooms, give prior notice of material you wish to consult. In search rooms, use official call slips to ask for material, after using indexes, to identify items required. The items will be brought to your seat. All baggage must be left at reception. No smoking, eating, drinking. No ink or ball-point pens allowed.
Postal enquiries accepted if specific, eg. will of one person, or sources for a subject. Also requests for photocopies if readily identifiable.
Search fees may be charged, and photocopies will be charged for.
Open: Mon.-Fri. 9am-4.45pm, except holidays, but arrive before 10 a.m. to be sure of a seat in summer months. The Historical Search Room is closed to the public for stocktaking the first two weeks of November, with the West Search Room closing the following week. (1/93)

Shetland Archives, 44 King Harald Street, Lerwick ZE1 0EQ, Tel.0595-3535, ext. 269, Fax.0595-6533.
Holdings: Census microfilm 1841-1891 for all Shetland, plus printed statistical reports for all years.
Holds returns for island of Fetlar, 1821 and 1831 (numbers only, but more detailed than official census);Census of parish of Mid and South Yell, mid-1830's, recorded by session clerk and containing all names of families, ages, occupations and addresses; complete list of Tingwall parish, 1785, names, ages & addresses, compiled as assessment for building of new church; Population Roll for distribution of charity meal and bread, 1804, some 1802, heads of families named;List of residents of Delting & Northmavine, 1808-15,1825-35.
Charges: none. Only basic enquiries answered by post. Contact in advance of visits preferable but not essential.
Open: Mon.-Thu., 9am-1pm, 2pm-5pm; Friday 9am-1pm, 2pm-4pm. Saturday closed. (10/93)

Shetland Library, Lower Hillhead, Lerwick ZE1 0EL, Tel.0595-3868, Fax.0595-4430.
No census microfilm, holds typescript copy of a Government Distribution of charity meal and bread in Shetland, which includes a population roll (mostly 1804, some 1802). Also typescript lists of residents of Delting and North Mavine areas, years 1808-1815 & 1825-1835. (10/93)

Skye: Clan Donald Centre, Armadale, Ardvasar, Isle of Skye IV45 8RS, Tel.(library) 04714-389, Fax.04714-275.
Holdings: Microfilm of census 1841-91 for Skye and other Clan Donald areas in Inverness-shire and Argyllshire; OPRs for similar area; 1988 IGI for Scotland. Rent records for MacDonald estates in Skye.
The Centre is open Easter to October, 7 days per week; outwith this period by appointment only. Access to Library and Study Centre included in general entrance ticket. Day tickets (1993):Adult £3, concessions £2, family £8. Photocopies: A4-10p,A3-12p.
Research charges for postal enquiries: £10 plus VAT per hour. Access to the Archives restricted to members of the Clan Donald Lands Trust (£10 per annum). (1/93)

Stirling District Libraries. Stirling Central Library, Corn Exchange Road, Stirling FK8 2HX, Tel.0786-479000,ext.2106 or 0786-471293, Fax.0786-473094.
Holdings of census microfilm: 1841-1891 for Stirlingshire parishes of Airth, Alva, Baldernock, Balfron, Bothkennar, Buchanan, Campsie, Denny, Drymen, Dunipace, Falkirk, Fintry, Gargunnock, Killearn, Kilsyth, Kippen, Larbert, Logie, Muiravonside, Polmont, St. Ninians, Slamannan, Stirling, Strathblane. All parishes of Perthshire are held for 1841 & 1851, and some also for later years.
Telephone in advance to ensure that a microfilm reader will be available.
Charges for postal enquiries: first half-hour of staff

time free, thereafter £10 per hour payable in advance. Photocopies:A4 - 10p. (2/93)

Strathclyde Regional Archives, incorporating Glasgow City Archives, Mitchell Library, North Street, Glasgow G3 7DN. Tel.041-227-2405.
Census microfilm is held by Glasgow District Libraries (see entry), and see leaflet, "Tracing your ancestors: Mitchell Library & Archive Sources". Recently purchased: Census microfilm for Argyll and Bute, 1841-1891.
Holds 1821 draft census for Lesmahagow [CO1/47/151]. Many other name lists held. General leaflet on the archives.
Open: Mon.-Thur. 9.30am-4.45pm, Fri. 9.30am-4pm.
See also: Ayr sub-office. (2/93)

Stirling University Library - No census material.

Strathclyde University Archives, 16 Richmond Street, Glasgow G1 1XQ, Tel.041-552-4400, ext.2318 - No census material. Holds records of the institution and its antecedents (e.g. Anderson's Institution, 1796-1887; Glasgow Mechanics' Institution, 1823-1887; Alan Glen's School; Glasgow Athenaeum; Technical College, etc.). Apart from a few earlier survivals, student records do not pre-date session 1888/89.
Postal enquiries welcomed and usually answered within a week of receipt.
Charge for searches in records arising from postal or other enquiries and exceeding one hour's duration: £15 per hour. Photocopies: up to A4-20p, over A4-40p. Charges for photographic copies of university copyright items: from £15 plus VAT.
Open: Mon.-Fri.9-5, by appointment. (1/93)

Strathkelvin District Libraries. Reference Department, William Patrick Library, Camphill Avenue, Kirkintilloch, Glasgow G66 1DW, Tel.041-776-0758.
Holdings of census microfilm: Baldernock, Cadder, Campsie, Kirkintilloch, (1841-1891); Airth, Alva, (1861-81); Balfron, Buchanan, Kilmaronock, (1841-81); Bonhill, Cumbernauld, Fintry, Gorbals, Govan, Killearn, Kilsyth, Kippen, Strathblane, (1851); Bothkennar, Denny, (1841,61-81); Cambuslang, Dunipace, (1841,61,71) Cambusnethan, Carluke, Luss, (1841,61); Carmichael, Carmunnock,(1841); Drymen,(1841-71); Dumbarton, (1841,71); New/East Kilpatrick, (1841-61); Old/West Kilpatrick, Roseneath, Row, (1861).
List of Householders, Cadder parish, 1797; Directories of Bishopbriggs starting 1848. Voters' rolls of Kirkintilloch 1839-44, 1872-1901.
Free leaflet on local history services. Postal enquiries accepted, if not too involved. Personal callers get preference. No charges.
Open: Mon.,Tue.,Thu.,Fri.,9.30am - 8pm; Wed. 9.30am - 1pm, 2pm-5pm; Sat. 9.30am - 1pm. (2/93)

Tayside Regional Archives. See: Dundee District Council.

West Lothian District Libraries - Wellpark, Marjoribanks Street, Bathgate, West Lothian EH48 1AN, Tel.0506-52866, Fax.0506-631563.
Holdings of Census microfilm: 1841-1891 for all parishes within West Lothian - both the old County and the present District.
"West Lothian Hearth Tax", ed. by Duncan Adamson, Scottish Record Society, 1981.
Postal enquiries accepted if specific dates and places given. Personal callers welcome, to do their own research. No charges. (1/93)

Western Isles Islands Council. Stornoway Library, Keith St., Stornoway, Isle of Lewis PA87 2QG, Tel.0851-703064, Fax.0851-705657.
Holdings of census microfilm at Stornoway: 1841-1891 for Isles of Lewis, Harris, North Uist, Benbecula, South Uist, Barra.
Holdings at Community Library, Sgoil lionacleit, Liniclate, Isle of Benbecula PA88 5PJ: census microfilm 1841-1891 for Isles of Harris, North Uist, Benbecula, South Uist, Barra.
Personal callers welcomed at both. Postal enquiries may be referred to a professional genealogist. (2/93)

NOTES

NOTES